THE BOOK OF
USELESS
INFORMATION

THE BOOK OF
USELESS
INFORMATION

NOEL BOTHAM AND THE
USELESS INFORMATION SOCIETY

A PERIGEE BOOK

THE BERKLEY PUBLISHING GROUP
Published by the Penguin Group
Penguin Group (USA) Inc.
375 Hudson Street, New York, New York 10014, USA
Penguin Group (Canada), 90 Eglinton Avenue East, Suite 700, Toronto, Ontario M4P 2Y3,
Canada (a division of Pearson Penguin Canada Inc.)
Penguin Books Ltd., 80 Strand, London WC2R 0RL, England
Penguin Group Ireland, 25 St. Stephen's Green, Dublin 2, Ireland
(a division of Penguin Books Ltd.)
Penguin Group (Australia), 250 Camberwell Road, Camberwell, Victoria 3124, Australia
(a division of Pearson Australia Group Pty. Ltd.)
Penguin Books India Pvt. Ltd., 11 Community Centre, Panchsheel Park,
New Delhi—110 017, India
Penguin Group (NZ), Cnr. Airborne and Rosedale Roads, Albany, Auckland 1310,
New Zealand (a division of Pearson New Zealand Ltd.)
Penguin Books (South Africa) (Pty.) Ltd., 24 Sturdee Avenue, Rosebank,
Johannesburg 2196, South Africa

Penguin Books Ltd., Registered Offices: 80 Strand, London WC2R 0RL, England

This book is an original publication of The Berkley Publishing Group.

While the author has made every effort to provide accurate telephone numbers and Internet
addresses at the time of publication, neither the publisher nor the author assumes any responsibility
for errors, or for changes that occur after publication. Further, publisher does not have any control
over and does not assume any responsibility for author or third-party websites or their content.

THE BOOK OF USELESS INFORMATION

Copyright © 2006 by Noel Botham.
Cover art by Getty Images.
Cover design by Ben Gibson.
Text design by Tiffany Estreicher.

First edition: July 2006

Perigee trade paperback ISBN: 0-399-53269-2

An application to register this book for cataloging has been submitted to the Library of Congress.

PRINTED IN THE UNITED STATES OF AMERICA

10   9   8

Members of The Useless Information Society

Chairman
NOEL BOTHAM
General Secretary
KEITH WATERHOUSE
Beadle
KENNY CLAYTON
Chaplain
FATHER MICHAEL SEED
MICHAEL DILLON
BRIAN HITCHEN
ALASDAIR LONG
TIM WOODWARD
RICHARD LITTLEJOHN
STEVE WALSH
STRUAN RODGER
GAVIN HANS-HAMILTON
ASHLEY LUFF

SUGGS
MIKE MALLOY
MICHAEL BOOTH
JOHN PAYNE
BARRY PALIN
JOSEPH CONNOLLY
TONY COBB
JOHN McENTEE
JOHN BLAKE
JOHN ROBERTS
BILL HAGGARTY
CHARLES LOWE
JOHN KING
KEN STOTT
RICHARD CORRIGAN
CONNER WALSH
JOHN TAYLOR

Contents

INTRODUCTION

INTRODUCTION

OH, but just how useless is useless? There, as Shakespeare observes in Act III, Scene I, of *The Oxford Dictionary of Quotations*, is the rub.

For instance, the news that flamingos can only eat with their heads upside down, while of more than passing interest to a female flamingo teaching her fledglings to eat up their shrimp, is of little use to a human being trained to sit up at a table and employ a knife and fork. Yet suppose someone made one a present of a flamingo, and it persisted in eating with its head upside down. You could spend a fortune on vet bills before learning that, in flamingo circles, that is the way it is done.

So we have to tread carefully. There have to be checks and balances. At our Useless Information Society summit meetings, we have these in the form of our formidable resident beadle, the distinguished jazz musician Kennie Clayton. If Mr. Beadle Clayton judges that an item may be put to use in the community, he solemnly bangs his ceremonial staff and it is ruled out of order. There is no appeal, although barracking and cries of "Rubbish!" are permitted.

An exception is sometimes made of material that may be of use to a biographer. Thus, when I learned from a newspaper cutting that Marilyn Monroe had six toes, I eagerly produced this nugget at the next Useless Information soirée in the confident belief that, with so many Marilyn biographers still trawling, it would get under the net. So it proved. What I hadn't bargained for was that one of our more pedantic members—and we have a few— would seek to have the item barred on purely arithmetical grounds, on the basis that in total she must have had eleven toes at least.

The only other transgression is that of being boring. At the society's earliest meetings, a few members misunderstood the nature of uselessness and came up with such conversation-stoppers as that the Mississippi is 1,171 miles long or, for those who prefer it, 1,884 kilometers. We useless information aficionados are not interested in the length of rivers, a fact that is traditionally conveyed to the offender with elaborate yawns and shouts of "Boring!" Tell us, however, that in the Nuuanu Valley of Honolulu there is a river that flows upward, and our eyes light up.

Mr. Gradgrind, in the same volume as the Bard's "There's the rub" gag, observes, "Facts alone are wanted in life." That is the policy of The Useless Information Society. It could be our motto.

But there are facts and *facts*. Useless information, as may be judged from this modest volume, is not in the same category as trivia, as in Trivial Pursuit. We do not care about any of that *Guinness World Records* kind of stuff. All our information has to pass the "Not a Lot of People Know That" test, preceded by gasps of surprise and, in extreme cases, followed by wild applause.

If we can send our fellow members home with their heads reeling under the weight of a cornucopia of entirely useless and out-of-the-way facts, then our deliberations will not have been in vain.

Keith Waterhouse

THE USELESS
INFORMATION MASCOT

It is estimated that millions of trees are planted by for-getful squirrels.

Squirrels can climb trees faster than they can run on the ground.

Squirrels may live fifteen or twenty years in captivity, but their life span in the wild is often only about one year. They fall prey to disease, malnutrition, predators, cars, and humans.

A squirrel cannot contract or carry the rabies virus.

THE BOOK OF
USELESS
INFORMATION

HALL OF FAME

HAIL TO THE CHIEFS

All U.S. presidents have worn glasses; some of them just didn't like to be seen wearing them in public.

There has never been a president from the Air Force or Marine Corps, although Ronald Reagan was in the Army Air Corps.

More presidents have been born in the state of Virginia than in any other state.

No president has been an only child.

The only three U.S. presidents who ever had to deal with real or impending impeachment—Andrew Johnson, Richard Nixon, and Bill Clinton—all have names that are euphemisms for "penis"—Johnson, Dick, and Willie.

David Rice Atchinson was president of the United States for exactly one day.

☙ CURIOUS GEORGE

George Washington is the only man whose birthday is a legal holiday in every state as of a few years ago.

George Washington grew marijuana in his garden.

George Washington was deathly afraid of being buried alive. After he died, he wanted to be laid out for three days just to be sure he was dead.

George Washington's false teeth were made of whale bone.

George Washington had to borrow money to go to his own inauguration.

Thomas Jefferson anonymously submitted design plans for the White House. They were rejected. He was the first president to be inaugurated in Washington, D.C.

Thomas Jefferson, John Adams, and James Monroe all died on July 4. Jefferson and Adams died at practically the same minute of the same day.

John Quincy Adams owned a pet alligator, which he kept in the East Room of the White House.

John Quincy Adams took his last skinny dip in the Potomac on his seventy-ninth birthday.

Andrew Jackson was the only president to believe that the world is flat.

The longest inaugural address by a U.S. president was given by William Henry Harrison. It was one hour, forty-five minutes long during an intense snowstorm. One month later, he died of pneumonia.

John Tyler had fifteen children.

Millard Fillmore's mother feared he may have been mentally retarded.

James Buchanan is said to have had the neatest handwriting of all the presidents. He was the only unmarried president.

Andrew Johnson was the only self-educated tailor. He is the only president to make his own clothes and those of his cabinet.

Ulysses S. Grant had the boyhood nickname "Useless."

🌰 HONEST ABE

Abraham Lincoln had a wart on his face.

Abraham Lincoln's mother died when the family dairy cow ate poisonous mushrooms and Mrs. Lincoln drank the milk.

Abraham Lincoln had a nervous breakdown in 1836.

Abraham Lincoln's famous Gettysburg Address consisted of just 272 words.

Before winning the presidential election in 1860, Abraham Lincoln lost eight elections for various offices.

A short time before Abraham Lincoln's assassination, he dreamed he was going to die, and he related his dream to the Senate. He died in the same bed that had been occupied by his assassin, John Wilkes Booth. His ghost is said to haunt the White House.

The annual White House Easter egg roll was started by Rutherford B. Hayes in 1878.

James Garfield could write Latin with one hand and Greek with the other—simultaneously!

Grover Cleveland was a draft dodger. He hired someone to enter the service in his place, for which he was ridiculed by his political opponent, James G. Blaine. It was soon discovered, however, that Blaine had done the same thing himself.

🌰 TEDDY TIDBITS

In 1812, after being shot in the chest, Theodore Roosevelt finished a speech he was delivering before he accepted any medical help.

Theodore Roosevelt was the first to announce to the world that Maxwell House coffee is "Good to the last drop."

Theodore Roosevelt wrote thirty-seven books.

Theodore Roosevelt's mother and first wife died on the same day in 1884. He himself died from an infected tooth.

William Taft got stuck in his bathtub on his Inauguration Day and had to be pried out by his attendants. He had a special, reinforced steel dining chair.

Woodrow Wilson wrote all of his speeches in longhand. He is the only president who has held a Ph.D. degree.

Herbert Hoover was the first U.S. president to have a telephone in his office.

When First Lady Eleanor Roosevelt received an alarming number of threatening letters soon after her husband became president at the height of the Depression, the Secret Service insisted that she carry a pistol in her purse.

Harry Truman's middle name was just S and was not short for anything. His parents could not decide between two different names beginning with S.

John F. Kennedy could read four newspapers in twenty minutes.

John F. Kennedy's rocking chair was auctioned off for $442,000.

Pluto, the astrological sign for death, was directly above Dallas when JFK was born.

Lyndon B. Johnson was the first president of the United States to wear contact lenses.

Richard Nixon left instructions for "California, Here I Come" to be the last piece of music played (slowly and softly) were he to die in office.

Richard Nixon's favorite drink was a dry martini.

Richard Nixon was the first U.S. president to visit Moscow.

Gerald Ford was once a male model.

Jimmy Carter is a speed reader (two thousand words per minute).

Jimmy Carter was the first U.S. president born in a hospital. He had an operation for hemorrhoids while he was in office.

REAGANISMS

Ronald Reagan once wore a Nazi uniform while acting in a film during his Hollywood days.

Ronald Reagan married his first wife, Jane Wyman, at Forest Lawn Cemetery in Glendale, California.

Ronald Reagan sent out the Army photographer who first discovered Marilyn Monroe.

Ronald Reagan was the only divorced president, and he was the only president to be head of a labor union.

Bill Clinton was the first left-handed U.S. president to serve two terms.

CRIMINAL MINDS

Al Capone's famous scars (which earned him the nickname "Scarface") were from an attack. The brother of a girl he had insulted attacked him with a knife, leaving him with three distinctive scars.

Al Capone's business card said he was a used furniture dealer. His brother was a town sheriff.

While in Alcatraz, Al Capone was inmate 85.

Behram, an Indian thug, holds the record for most murders by a single individual. He strangled 931 people between 1790 and 1840 with a piece of yellow and white cloth called a ruhmal. The most by a woman is 610, by Countess Erzsebet Bathory of Hungary.

Mass murderer Charles Manson recorded an album called *Lie*.

Benito Mussolini would ward off the evil eye by touching his testicles.

Fidel Castro was once a star baseball player for the University of Havana in the 1940s.

Leon Trotsky, the seminal Russian Communist, was assassinated in Mexico with an ice pick.

Lee Harvey Oswald's body tag was auctioned off for $6,600.

Josef Stalin's left foot had webbed toes, and his left arm was noticeably shorter than his right arm.

DER FÜHRER

Adolf Hitler was *Time*'s Man of the Year in 1938.

Hitler's great-great-grandmother was a Jewish maid.

Hitler had planned to change the name of Berlin to Germania.

Hitler refused to shake Jesse Owens's hand at the 1936 Olympics because he was black.

Hitler was claustrophobic. The elevator leading to his eagles' nest in the Austrian Alps was mirrored so it would appear larger and more open.

THE OTHER KENNEDYS

Robert Kennedy was killed in the Ambassador Hotel, the same hotel that housed Marilyn Monroe's first modeling agency.

While at Harvard University, Edward Kennedy was suspended for cheating on a Spanish exam.

LOUIS, LOUIS

Louis IV of France had a stomach the size of two regular stomachs.

Louis XIV bathed once a year. He had forty personal wigmakers and almost one thousand wigs.

THE ROYAL WE

The Queen of England has two birthdays—one real and one official.

The shortest British monarch was Charles I, who was four foot, nine inches.

Prince Harry and Prince William are uncircumcised.

Catherine the Great relaxed by being tickled.

Princess Grace of Monaco was once on the board of 20th Century Fox.

The royal house of Saudi Arabia has close to ten thousand princes and princesses.

While performing her duties as queen, Cleopatra sometimes wore a fake beard.

King Tut's tomb contained four coffins. The third coffin was made from twenty-five hundred pounds of gold, and in today's market is worth approximately $13 million.

Peter the Great executed his wife's lover and forced her to keep her lover's head in a jar of alcohol in her bedroom.

The German kaiser Wilhelm II had a withered arm and often hid the fact by posing with his hand resting on a sword or by holding a glove.

The Mongol emperor Genghis Khan's original name was Temuji. He started out as a goatherder.

Alexander the Great was an epileptic. He was tutored by Aristotle.

Augustus Caesar had achluophobia—the fear of sitting in the dark.

Catherine de Medici was the first woman in Europe to use tobacco. She took it in a mixture of snuff.

GOD SAVE THE QUEEN

Six of Queen Victoria's grandchildren were married to rulers of countries—England, Russia, Germany, Sweden, Norway, and Romania. Queen Victoria's native language was German.

Queen Victoria eased the discomfort of her menstrual cramps by having her doctor supply her with marijuana.

The first thing Queen Victoria did after her coronation was to remove her bed from her mother's room.

One of Queen Victoria's children gave her a bustle for Christmas that played "God Save the Queen" when she sat down.

All of Queen Anne's seventeen children died before she did.

Anne Boleyn, Queen Elizabeth I's mother, had six fingers on one hand.

Elizabeth I suffered from anthophobia—a fear of roses.

Princess Anne competed in the 1976 Summer Olympics.

Queen Berengaria (1191 c.e.) of England never lived in nor visited England.

ARTISTIC ENDEAVORS

The famous painting *Whistler's Mother* was once bought from a pawn shop.

The *Mona Lisa* was completed in 1503. It was stolen from the Louvre on August 21, 1911.

A Flemish artist is responsible for the world's smallest painting in history. It is a picture of a miller and his mill, and it was painted onto a grain of corn.

Artist Constantino Brumidi fell from the dome of the U.S. Capitol while painting a mural around the rim. He died four months later.

Leonardo da Vinci spent twelve years painting the *Mona Lisa's* lips. He could also write with one hand and draw with the other at the same time.

On a trip to the South Sea Islands, French painter Paul Gauguin stopped off briefly in Central America, where he worked as a laborer on the Panama Canal.

Salvador Dalí once arrived at an art exhibition in a limousine filled with turnips.

When young and impoverished, Pablo Picasso kept warm by burning his own paintings.

Michelangelo carved the famed Medici tombs in Florence.

🌰 GOGH CRAZY

Vincent van Gogh decided to become an artist when he was twenty-seven years old.

Van Gogh cut off his left ear. His *Self-Portrait with Bandaged Ear* shows the right one bandaged because he painted his mirror image.

During his entire life, van Gogh sold only one painting, *Red Vineyard at Arles*.

Van Gogh committed suicide while painting *Wheat Field with Crows*.

BRAINIACS

Alexander Graham Bell made a talking doll that said "Mama" when he was a young boy in Scotland. He never telephoned his wife or mother. They were both deaf.

Aristotle thought blood cooled the brain.

Despite his great scientific and artistic achievement, Leonardo da Vinci was most proud of his ability to bend iron with his bare hands.

Jeremy Bentham, a British philosopher who died in 1832, left his entire estate to the London Hospital, provided that his body was allowed to preside over its board meetings. His skeleton was clothed and fitted with a wax mask of his face. It was present at the meeting for ninety-two years and can still be viewed there.

Thomas Edison had a collection of more than five thousand birds. He once saved a boy from the path of an oncoming locomotive.

NEWTONIAN PRINCIPLES

Isaac Newton was an ordained priest in the Church of England.

Isaac Newton was only twenty-three years old when he discovered the law of universal gravitation.

Isaac Newton dropped out of school when he was a teenager.

Isaac Newton was a Member of Parliament.

Nobody knows where Voltaire's body is. It was stolen in the nineteenth century and has never been recovered. The theft was discovered in 1864, when the tomb was opened and found empty.

Sigmund Freud had a morbid fear of ferns.

Socrates committed suicide by drinking the poison hemlock. He left no writings of his own.

At age sixteen, Confucius was a corn inspector.

RELATIVITY SPEAKING

Albert Einstein couldn't speak fluently when he was nine. His parents thought he might be mentally retarded.

In 1921, Einstein was awarded the Nobel Prize in Physics for his work with the photoelectric effect.

Einstein was offered the presidency of Israel in 1952.

When Einstein was inducted as an American, he attended the ceremony without socks.

Einstein's last words were in German. Because the attending nurse did not understand German, his last words will never be known.

THAT EXPLAINS IT

Hitler and Napoleon both had only one testicle.

A LITTLE EGO

Napoleon Bonaparte was afraid of cats.

Napoleon conducted his battle plans in a sandbox.

Napoleon favored mathematicians and physical scientists but excluded humanists from his circle, believing them to be troublemakers.

Napoleon had his servants wear his boots to break them in before he wore them.

LARGER THAN LIFE

Attila the Hun was a dwarf. Pepin the Short, Aesop, Gregory the Tours, Charles III of Naples, and the Pasha Hussain were all shorter than three and a half feet tall.

BIG BEN

Benjamin Franklin wanted the turkey, not the eagle, to be the U.S. national bird.

Benjamin Franklin was the first head of the United States Post Office.

Benjamin Franklin's peers did not give him the assignment of writing the Declaration of Independence because they feared he would conceal a joke in it.

DID IT RUN WINDOWS?

Bill Gates's first business was Traff-O-Data, a company that created machines that recorded the number of cars passing a given point on a road.

WE LIKE TO CALL HIM "ECCENTRIC"

Henry Ford believed in reincarnation and flatly stated that history is bunk.

GLOBETROTTERS

Marco Polo was born on the Croatian island of Korcula (pronounced *Kor-chu-la*).

Christopher Columbus had blond hair.

American explorer Richard Byrd once spent five months alone in Antarctica.

Harry Houdini was the first person to fly an airplane on the continent of Australia.

THAT'S ENTERTAINMENT

A ROSE BY ANY OTHER NAME

Bruce Willis's real name is Walter.

Cher's real name is Cherilyn La Pierre.

Hulk Hogan's real name is Terry Bollea.

Ice Cube's real name is O'Shea Jackson.

John Wayne's real name was Marion Morrison.

Judy Garland's real name was Frances Gumm.

Tom Cruise's real name is Thomas Mapother.

Tina Turner's real name is Annie Mae Bullock.

Vanilla Ice's real name is Robert Van Winkle.

Albert Brooks's real name is Albert Einstein.

Ralph Lauren's real name is Ralph Lifshitz.

Jim Carrey's middle name is Eugene.

Keanu Reeves's first name means "cool breeze over the mountains" in Hawaiian.

Cleo and Caesar were the early stage names of Cher and Sonny Bono.

FAMILY TIES

Warren Beatty and Shirley MacLaine are brother and sister.

Sophia Loren's sister was once married to the son of the Italian dictator Benito Mussolini.

Julie Nixon, daughter of Richard Nixon, married David Eisenhower, grandson of Dwight Eisenhower.

Humphrey Bogart was related to Princess Diana, according to U.S. genealogists.

Tom Hanks is related to Abraham Lincoln.

I'M READY FOR MY CLOSE-UP

Andy Garcia was a Siamese, or conjoined, twin.

Arnold Schwarzenegger bought the first Hummer manufactured for civilian use, in 1992. The vehicle weighed in at 6,300 pounds and was seven feet wide. He also paid $772,500 for President John F. Kennedy's golf clubs at a 1996 auction.

Tommy Lee Jones and Vice President Al Gore were freshmen roommates at Harvard.

Sarah Bernhardt played a thirteen-year-old Juliet when she was seventy years old.

Although he starred in many gangster films, James Cagney started his career as a chorus boy.

As a child, Jodie Foster appeared in Coppertone commercials.

Bruce Lee was so fast that his films actually had to be slowed down so audiences could see his moves.

David Niven and George Lazenby were the only two actors who played James Bond only once.

The first actress to appear on a postage stamp was Grace Kelly.

Tom Cruise at one time wanted to be a priest.

Peter Falk, who played Columbo, has a glass eye.

Peter Mayhew, who played Chewbacca in the first three *Star Wars* movies, was a hospital porter in London before starring as the Wookie.

Shirley Temple made $1 million by age ten.

Keanu Reeves once managed a pasta shop in Toronto.

Mae West did not utter her infamous line, "Is that a gun in your pocket or are you just happy to see me?" until her last film, *Sextette*. It had been floating around for years and has always been attributed to her, but its exact origins are unknown.

Mae West was once dubbed "the statue of Libido."

Melanie Griffith's mother is actress Tippi Hedren, best known for her lead role in Alfred Hitchcock's *The Birds*.

Alfred Hitchcock did not have a belly button.

Rita Moreno is the first and only entertainer to have received all four of America's top entertainment industry awards: the Oscar, the Emmy, the Tony, and the Grammy.

James Doohan, who played Lt. Commander Montgomery Scott on *Star Trek*, was missing his entire middle finger on his right hand.

In 1953, Marilyn Monroe appeared as the first *Playboy* centerfold.

Jack Nicholson appeared on *The Andy Griffith Show* twice.

Telly Savalas and Louis Armstrong died on their birthdays.

Jill St. John, Jack Klugman, Diana Ross, Carol Burnett, and Cher have all worn braces as adults.

Orson Welles is buried in an olive orchard on a ranch owned by his friend, matador Antonio Ordonez, in Seville, Spain.

Kathleen Turner was the voice of Jessica Rabbit in the movie *Who Framed Roger Rabbit?* Amy Irving was her singing voice.

James Dean died in a Porsche Spyder.

Sylvia Miles had the shortest performance ever nominated for an Oscar with her role in *Midnight Cowboy*. Her entire role lasted only six minutes.

Katharine Hepburn is the only person to win four Oscars for Best Actress.

Clark Gable used to shower more than four times a day.

Elizabeth Taylor has appeared on the cover of *Life* magazine more than anyone else.

MAKE 'EM LAUGH

Charlie Chaplin started in show business at age five. He was so popular during the 1920s and 1930s he received more than 73,000 letters in just two days during a visit to London.

Charlie Chaplin once won third prize in a Charlie Chaplin look-alike contest.

Howdy Doody had forty-eight freckles. His twin brother was named Double Doody.

Dan Aykroyd's cone head from *Saturday Night Live* was auctioned off for $2,200.

Roseanne Barr used to be an opening act for Julio Iglesias.

In high school, Robin Williams was voted the least likely to succeed.

Bill Cosby was the first black man to win an Emmy for Best Actor.

I WANNA HOLD YOUR HAND

The Beatles featured two left-handed members: Paul, whom everyone saw holding his Hoffner bass left-handed, and Ringo, whose left-handedness is at least partially to blame for his "original" drumming style.

The Beatles performed their first U.S. concert in Carnegie Hall.

The Beatles song "A Day in the Life" ends with a note sustained for forty seconds.

The Beatles song "Dear Prudence" was written about Mia Farrow's sister, Prudence, when she wouldn't come out and play with Mia and The Beatles at a religious retreat in India.

The license plate number on the Volkswagen that appeared on the cover of The Beatles' album *Abbey Road* is 281F.

"When I'm Sixty-Four" was the first song to be recorded for the *Sgt. Pepper* album. "Within You Without You" was the last.

When John Lennon divorced Julian Lennon's mother, Paul McCartney composed "Hey Jude" to cheer up Julian.

John Lennon's first girlfriend was named Thelma Pickles.

John Lennon's middle name was Winston.

Ringo Starr was born during a World War II air raid.

ONE-MAN SHOW

An eighteenth-century German named Matthew Birchinger, known as The Little Man of Nuremberg, played four musical instruments, including the bagpipes; was an expert calligrapher; and was the most famous stage magician of his day. He performed tricks with the cup and balls that have never been explained. Yet Birchinger had no hands, legs, or thighs, and he was shorter than twenty-nine inches tall.

INSTRUMENTAL VERSION

The bagpipe was originally made from the whole skin of a dead sheep. Carnegie Mellon University offers bagpiping as a major.

A penny whistle has six finger holes.

The tango originated as a dance between two men for partnering practice.

The harmonica is the world's most popular instrument.

There are more than thirty-three thousand radio stations around the world.

A single violin is made of seventy separate pieces of wood.

Glass flutes do not expand with humidity, so their owners are spared the nuisance of tuning them.

In 1990, there were an estimated seventy-five thousand accordionists in the United States.

The first U.S. discotheque was the Whisky A Go-Go in Los Angeles.

Gandhi took dance and music lessons in his late teens.

CLASSICALLY SPEAKING

More than one hundred descendants of Johann Sebastian Bach have been cathedral organists.

When Beethoven was a child, he made such a poor impression on his music teachers that he was pronounced hopeless as a composer.

Beethoven's *Fifth* was the first symphony to include trombones.

Every time Beethoven sat down to write music, he poured ice water over his head.

Mozart's real name was Johannes Chrysostomus Wolfgangus Theophilus Mozart.

Mozart wrote the nursery rhyme "Twinkle Twinkle, Little Star" at the age of five.

Mozart is buried in an unmarked pauper's grave.

PLAY THAT FUNKY MUSIC

At age forty-seven, The Rolling Stones' bassist, Bill Wyman, began a relationship with thirteen-year-old Mandy Smith, with her mother's blessing. Six years later, they were married, but the marriage only lasted a year. Not long after, Bill's thirty-year-old son, Stephen, married Mandy's mother, age forty-six. That made Stephen a stepfather to his former stepmother. If Bill and Mandy had remained married, Stephen would have been his father's father-in-law and his own grandfather.

The music hall entertainer Nosmo King derived his stage name from a NO SMOKING sign.

Jonathan Houseman Davis, lead singer of Korn, was born a Presbyterian but converted to Catholicism because his mother wanted to marry his stepfather in a Catholic church.

Nick Mason is the only member of Pink Floyd to appear on all the band's albums.

The naked baby on the cover of Nirvana's album *Nevermind* is named Spencer Eldon.

The 1980s song "Rosanna" was written about actress Rosanna Arquette.

The B-52s were named after a 1950s hairdo.

The band Duran Duran got their name from a character in the 1968 Jane Fonda movie *Barbarella*.

The Beach Boys formed in 1961.

The bestselling Christmas single of all time is Bing Crosby's "White Christmas."

The first CD pressed in the United States was Bruce Springsteen's *Born in the USA*.

The Grateful Dead were once called The Warlocks.

The Mamas and Papas were once called The Mugwumps.

The only member of the band ZZ Top to not have a beard has the last name Beard.

There is a band named A Life-Threatening Buttocks Condition.

The song with the longest title is "I'm a Cranky Old Yank in a Clanky Old Tank on the Streets of Yokohama with My Honolulu Mama Doin' Those Beat-O, Beat-O Flat-On-My-Seat-O, Hirohito Blues," written by Hoagy Carmichael. He later claimed the song title ended with "Yank" and the rest was a joke.

Tommy James got the inspiration to write his number-one hit "Mony Mony" while he was in a New York hotel looking at the Mutual of New York building's neon sign flashing repeatedly: M-O-N-Y.

ABBA got its name by taking the first letter from each of the band members' names (Agnetha, Bjorn, Benny, and Anni-frid).

The opera singer Enrico Caruso practiced in the bath, while accompanied by a pianist in a nearby room.

Enrico Caruso and Roy Orbison were the only tenors in the twentieth century capable of hitting the note E over high C.

The song "I Am the Walrus" by John Lennon was inspired by a two-tone police siren.

In every show Tom Jones and Harvey Schmidt (*The Fantasticks*) wrote, there was at least one song about rain.

Aerosmith's "Dude Looks Like a Lady" was written about Vince Neil of Mötley Crüe.

Andy Warhol created The Rolling Stones' emblem depicting the big tongue. It first appeared on the cover of the *Sticky Fingers* album.

"Happy Birthday to You" is the most often sung song in America.

The band Steely Dan got its name from a sexual device depicted in the book *Naked Lunch*.

Al Kooper played keyboards for Bob Dylan before he was famous.

🐚 LONG LIVE THE KING

Elvis Presley had a twin brother named Garon, who died at birth. Elvis's middle name was spelled Aron in honor of his brother.

Elvis loved to eat meatloaf. He weighed 230 pounds at the time of his death.

Elvis failed his music class in school.

Elvis never gave an encore.

Elvis was once appointed Special Agent of the Bureau of Narcotics and Dangerous Drugs. According to Elvis's autopsy, he had ten different drugs in his body at the time of his death.

Frank Sinatra was once quoted as saying that rock 'n' roll was only played by "cretinous goons."

Jim Morrison of The Doors was the first rock star to be arrested onstage.

Mr. Mojo Risin is an anagram for Jim Morrison.

Jimi Hendrix, Janis Joplin, and Jim Morrison were all twenty-seven years old when they died.

Karen Carpenter's doorbell chimed the first six notes of "We've Only Just Begun."

Madonna once did a commercial for Pepsi.

Mick Jagger attended the London School of Economics for two years.

Paul McCartney's mother was a midwife.

Shannon Hoon, the late lead singer of the group Blind Melon, was a backup singer for Guns N' Roses on their *Use Your Illusion I* album.

Sheryl Crow's two front teeth are fake. She knocked them out when she tripped onstage earlier in her career.

Michael Jackson is black.

ALSO KNOWN AS INTERMISSION

Breath, by Samuel Beckett, was first performed in April 1970. The play lasts thirty seconds and has no actors or dialogue.

DO NOT PASS GO

Since its introduction in February 1935, more than 150 million Monopoly board games have been sold worldwide.

Parker Brothers prints about $50 billion worth of Monopoly money in a year.

Every day, more money is printed for Monopoly than by the U.S. Treasury. The most money you can lose in one trip around the board (normal game rules, going to jail only once) is $26,040. The most money you can lose in one turn is $5,070.

Values on the Monopoly game board are the same today as they were in 1935.

The longest Monopoly game in a bathtub was ninety-nine hours long.

PLAY TO WIN

English gambling dens used to have employees whose job was to swallow the dice if the police arrived.

The word *checkmate* in chess comes from the Persian phrase *Shah-Mat*, which means "The king is dead."

According to Pope Innocent III, it was not a crime to kill someone after a game of chess.

Australia is considered the easiest continent to defend in the game Risk.

The Ouija board is named after the French and German words for "yes"—*oui* and *ja*.

Trivial Pursuit was invented by Canadians Scott Abbott and Chris Haney. They didn't want to pay the price for Scrabble, so they made up their own game.

Mario, of Super Mario Bros. fame, first appeared in the 1981 arcade game *Donkey Kong*. His original name was Jumpman, but that was changed to Mario to honor Nintendo of America, Inc.'s landlord, Mario Segali.

Westwood Studios' computer game *Command and Conquer* is the most successful war game series of all time, according to *Guinness World Records*.

MUPPET MOMENTS

Kermit the Frog was named after Kermit Scott, a child-hood friend of Jim Henson's, who became a professor of philosophy at Purdue University. Kermit has eleven points on the collar around his neck and is left-handed.

Miss Piggy's measurements are 27-20-36.

TV GUIDE

One in every four Americans has appeared on television.

Sitcom characters rarely say good-bye when they hang up the phone.

Daytime dramas are called soap operas because they were originally used to advertise soap powder. In America in the early days of television, advertisers would write stories around the use of their soap powder.

For many years, the globe on the NBC *Nightly News* spun in the wrong direction. On January 2, 1984, NBC finally set the world spinning in the proper direction.

When Patty Hearst was kidnapped, she was watching the TV show *The Magician*, starring Bill Bixby.

Of the six men who made up The Three Stooges over the years, only three of them were real brothers.

The first ever televised murder case aired December 5 through 9, 1955.

The *Love Boat*'s titular ship was named the *Pacific Princess*.

M*A*S*H MATTERS

M*A*S*H stood for Mobile Army Surgical Hospital.

Jamie Farr was the only member of the cast who actually served as a soldier in the Korean War.

Hawkeye's real name was Benjamin Franklin Pierce. He was played by Alan Alda.

Sixty point two percent of the U.S. TV audience watched the final episode of M*A*S*H in 1983.

There are as many as seventy-eight scenes in a single *X-Files* episode.

Gunsmoke was the top-rated series from 1957 to 1961.

The *Brady Brunch* kids went to elementary school at Dixie Canyon Elementary.

The characters of Bert and Ernie on *Sesame Street* were named after Bert the cop and Ernie the taxi driver in Frank Capra's *It's a Wonderful Life*.

The first crime mentioned in the first episode of *Hill Street Blues* was armed robbery.

Every episode of *Seinfeld* contains a Superman reference somewhere.

Mr. Munster's first name is Herman.

On *Roseanne*, DJ stood for David Jacob.

On *Gilligan's Island*, the professor's real name was Roy Hinkley, Mary Ann's last name was Summers, and Mrs. Howell's maiden name was Wentworth.

▟ LIVE LONG AND PROSPER

Mr. Spock was second in command of the Starship *Enterprise*. His blood type was T-negative.

As well as appearing on *Star Trek*, William Shatner, Leonard Nimoy, James Doohan, and George Takei have all appeared at one time or another on *The Twilight Zone*.

The mask used by Michael Myers in the original *Halloween* movie was actually a Captain Kirk mask painted white.

Captain Jean-Luc Picard's fish was named Livingston.

ANIMATION NATION

Yasser Arafat was addicted to watching television cartoons.

Boris Karloff is the narrator of the seasonal television special *How the Grinch Stole Christmas*.

Before Mickey Mouse, Felix the Cat was the most popular cartoon character. He was the first cartoon character to ever have been made into a balloon for a parade.

Bill Cosby created the cartoon characters Fat Albert and Weird Harold.

Cheryl Ladd (of *Charlie's Angels* fame) played the voice, both talking and singing, of Josie in the 1970s Saturday morning cartoon *Josie and the Pussycats*.

Dagwood Bumstead's dog is named Daisy.

Dennis the Menace's dog is named Gnasher.

Beetle from the comic strip *Beetle Bailey* and Lois from the comic strip *Hi and Lois* are brother and sister.

Marmaduke the cartoon dog is a Great Dane.

Of the four Teenage Mutant Ninja Turtles, all named after painters and/or sculptors, only Donatello does not come from the same time period as Leonardo, Michelangelo, and Raphael.

MEET THE FLINTSTONES

Wilma Flintstone's maiden name was Wilma Slaghoopal, and Betty Rubble's was Betty Jean McBricker.

The movie playing at the drive-in at the beginning of *The Flintstones* is called *The Monster*.

On *The Jetsons*, Jane is thirty-three years old, and her daughter Judy is eighteen.

Pokémon stands for "pocket monster."

Rocky Raccoon lives in the Black Hills of South Dakota.

The most common set of initials for Superman's friends and enemies is L.L.

🌰 RETURN TO SENDER

The Simpsons live at 742 Evergreen Terrace, Springfield. The Munsters live at 1313 Mockingbird Lane, Mockingbird Heights. The Flintstones live at 39 Stone Canyon Way, Bedrock.

Tony the Tiger was voiced by Thurl Ravenscroft.

Scooby-Doo's real first name is Scoobert. Shaggy's real name is Norville. Casey Kasem was the voice of Shaggy.

🌰 D'OH!

The Simpsons is the longest-running animated series on TV.

Matt Groening, creator of *The Simpsons*, incorporated his initials into the drawing of Homer. M is his hair, and G is his ear.

Patty and Selma smoke Laramie brand cigarettes.

GOING 'NUTS

Peanuts is the world's most read comic strip.

Charlie Brown's father is a barber.

Lucy and Linus have another little brother named Rerun. He sometimes plays left field on Charlie Brown's baseball team—when he can find it!

EAT MORE SPINACH

Elzie Crisler Segar created the comic strip character Popeye in 1919.

After the *Popeye* comic strip started in 1931, spinach consumption went up by 33 percent in the United States.

Popeye is five feet, six inches tall. He has an anchor tattooed on his arm.

Popeye's adopted son is named Swee'pea.

LOONEY TUNES

Mel Blanc, who voiced Bugs Bunny, was allergic to carrots.

Bugs Bunny first said "What's up, doc?" in the 1940 cartoon *A Wild Hare*.

The Looney Tunes theme song is actually called "The Merry-Go-Round Is Broken Down."

Tweety used to be a baby bird without feathers until the censors decided he looked naked.

WHEN YOU WISH UPON A STAR

Walt Disney named Mickey Mouse after Mickey Rooney, whose mother he dated for some time. Walt Disney originally supplied the voice for Mickey Mouse.

Mickey Mouse is known as "Topolino" in Italy. He was the first nonhuman to win an Oscar. His birthday is November 18.

Mickey Mouse's ears are always turned to the front, no matter which direction his head is pointing.

The Black Cauldron is the only PG-rated Disney animated feature.

Goofy has a wife, Mrs. Goofy, and one son, Goofy Jr.

Goofy actually started life as "Dippy Dawg," a combination of both Goofy and Pluto.

Donald Duck comics were banned in Finland because he doesn't wear pants.

Donald Duck's middle name is Fauntleroy. His sister is named Dumbella.

Peter Pan and *101 Dalmatians* are the only two classic Disney cartoon features in which both parents are present and don't die throughout the movie.

The Lion King is the top-grossing Disney movie of all time, with a domestic gross intake of $312 million.

In *Fantasia*, the sorcerer's name is Yensid—*Disney* spelled backward.

Walt Disney died of lung cancer.

Walt Disney's autograph bears no resemblance to the famous Disney logo.

CINEMA FIRSTS

The first real motion picture theater was called a nickelodeon—admission was a nickel—and opened in McKeesport, Pennsylvania, on June 19, 1905. The first motion picture shown there was *The Great Train Robbery*.

The first female monster to appear on the big screen was the Bride of Frankenstein.

The first James Bond movie was *Dr. No.*

The first word spoken by an ape in the movie *Planet of the Apes* is "Smile."

C3PO is the first character to speak in *Star Wars*.

Love Me Tender was Elvis Presley's first film.

Mrs. Claus's first name is Jessica in the movie *Santa Claus Is Coming to Town.*

The first time the "f-word" was spoken in a movie was by Marianne Faithfull in the 1968 film *I'll Never Forget Whatshisname*. In Brian De Palma's 1984 movie *Scarface*, the word is spoken 206 times—an average of once every 29 seconds.

WE ALL MAKE MISTAKES

During the chariot scene in *Ben-Hur,* a small red car can be seen in the distance.

In the film *Star Trek: First Contact,* when Picard shows Lilly she is orbiting Earth, Australia and Papua New Guinea are clearly visible . . . but New Zealand is missing.

In the movie *Now and Then,* when the girls are talking to the hippie and they get up to leave, Teeny puts out her cigarette twice.

If you pause *Saturday Night Fever* at the "How Deep Is Your Love" rehearsal scene, you will see the camera crew reflected in the dance hall mirror.

In 1976, Rodrigo's song "Guitar Concierto de Aranjuez" was number one in the United Kingdom for only three hours because of a computer error.

HOLLYWOOD INSIDER

When a film is in production, the last shot of the day is called the "martini shot"; the next-to-last one is called the "Abby Singer" after a famous assistant director.

Smithee is a pseudonym filmmakers use when they don't want their names to appear in the credits.

A "walla-walla" scene is one in which extras pretend to be talking in the background—when they say "walla-walla," it looks like they are actually having a conversation.

The Academy Award statue is named after a librarian's uncle. One day Margaret Herrick, librarian for the Academy of Motion Picture Arts and Sciences, made the remark that the statue looked like her uncle Oscar, and the name stuck.

In the early days of silent films, there was blatant thievery. Unscrupulous film companies would steal the film, reshoot a scene or two, and release it as a new production. To combat this, the Biograph Company put the company's trademark initials, AB, somewhere in every scene—on a door, a wall, or a window.

Ronald Reagan did a narration at the 1947 Academy Awards ceremony.

The second unit films movie shots that do not require the presence of actors.

Alfred Hitchcock never won an Academy Award for directing.

Because metal was scarce, the Academy Awards given out during World War II were made of wood.

A GALAXY FAR, FAR AWAY . . .

The actor who played Wedge in the original *Star Wars* trilogy has a famous nephew: actor Ewan McGregor, who plays young Obi-Wan in the new *Star Wars* trilogy.

Darth Vader is the only officer in the Imperial Forces who doesn't have a rank.

In the *Return of the Jedi* special edition, during the new Coruscant footage at the end of the film, a storm trooper can be seen being carried over the crowds.

Four people played Darth Vader: David Prowse was his body, James Earl Jones did the voice, Sebastian Shaw was his face, and a fourth person did his breathing.

Luke Skywalker's last name was changed at the last minute from Starkiller to make it less violent.

The name of Jabba the Hutt's pet spider monkey is Salacious Crumb.

YOU HAIRY APE

King Kong is the only movie to have its sequel (*Son of Kong*) released in the same year (1933).

King Kong was Adolf Hitler's favorite movie.

Skull Island is the jungle home of King Kong.

SHARK TALE

Bruce was the nickname of the mechanical shark used in the *Jaws* movies.

In the 1983 film *Jaws 3D*, the shark blows up. Some of the shark guts were stuffed E.T. dolls being sold at the time.

ENJOY THE SHOW

One of the many Tarzans, Karmuala Searlel, was mauled to death by a raging elephant on the set.

Debra Winger was the voice of E.T.

Dirty Harry's last name is Callahan.

In *Psycho*, Mrs. Bates's dress was periwinkle blue.

🃏 SHAKEN, NOT STIRRED

Felix Leiter is James Bond's CIA contact.

James Bond is known as "Mr. Kiss-Kiss-Bang-Bang" in Italy.

Jean-Claude Van Damme was the alien in the original *Predator* in almost all the jumping and climbing scenes.

More bullets were fired in *Starship Troopers* than in any other movie ever made.

The famous theme ostensibly from *Dragnet* was actually composed by Miklos Rozsa for the 1946 film noir classic *The Killers*.

Godzilla has made the covers of *Time* and *Newsweek*.

Gone With the Wind is the only Civil War epic ever filmed without a single battle scene.

The movie *Cleopatra*, starring Elizabeth Taylor, was banned from Egypt in 1963 because Taylor is a Jewish convert.

The movie *Clue* has three different endings. Each ending was randomly chosen for different theaters. All three endings are present on the DVD.

The movie *Paris, Texas* was banned in the city Paris, Texas, shortly after its box-office release.

The skyscraper in *Die Hard* is the Century Fox Tower.

The sound of E.T. walking was made by someone squishing her hands in jelly.

The word *mafia* was purposely omitted from the *Godfather* screenplay.

Dracula is the most filmed story of all time. *Dr. Jekyll and Mr. Hyde* is second, and *Oliver Twist* is third.

When the movie *The Wizard of Oz* first came out, it got bad reviews. The critics said it was stupid and uncreative.

THE NUMBERS GAME

Smokey the Bear's zip code is 20252.

Dirty Harry's badge number is 2211.

Sleeping Beauty slept one hundred years.

Approximately sixty circus performers have been shot from cannons. At last report, thirty-one of them have been killed.

There are twenty-two stars surrounding the mountain on the Paramount Pictures logo.

In 1938, Joe Shuster and Jerry Siegel sold all rights to the comic-strip character *Superman* to their publishers for $130.

The number of the trash compactor in *Star Wars* is 3263827.

Pulp Fiction cost $8 million to make. Of that amount, $5 million went to actors' salaries.

In an episode of *The Simpsons*, Sideshow Bob's criminal number is 24601, the same as the criminal number of Jean Valjean in *Les Misérables*.

All the clocks in the movie *Pulp Fiction* are stuck on 4:20.

The longest film ever released was **** by Andy Warhol, which lasted twenty-four hours. It proved, not surprisingly (except perhaps to its creator), an utter failure. It was withdrawn and re-released in a ninety-minute form as *The Loves of Ondine*.

The longest Hollywood kiss was from the 1941 film *You're in the Army Now*; it lasted three minutes and three seconds.

A Chinese checkerboard has 121 holes.

There are 225 spaces on a Scrabble board.

There are one hundred squares on a Snakes and Ladders board.

The total number of bridge hands possible is 54 octillion.

There are 311,875,200 five-card hands possible in a fifty-two-card deck of cards.

The wheel on the game show *Wheel of Fortune* is 102 inches in diameter.

John Travolta's white suit from *Saturday Night Fever* was auctioned off for $145,500; Judy Garland's ruby slippers for $165,000; Charlie Chaplin's hat and cane for $211,500; Elvis's jacket for $59,700; and John Lennon's glasses for $25,875.

THE LITERARY WORLD

PAGE TO SCREEN

Bambi was originally published in 1929 in German.

General Lew Wallace's best-seller *Ben-Hur* was the first work of fiction to be blessed by a pope.

The name for Oz in *The Wizard of Oz* was thought up when the author, L. Frank Baum, looked at his filing cabinet and saw A–N and O–Z, hence Oz.

THE USELESS INFORMATION BOOK CLUB

An estimated 2.5 million books will be shipped in the next twelve months with the wrong covers.

Louisa May Alcott, author of the classic *Little Women*, hated children. She only wrote the book because her publisher asked her to.

Susan Haswell Rowson was America's first bestselling novelist for her novel *Charlotte Goode*.

During his entire lifetime, Herman Melville's timeless classic of the sea, *Moby Dick*, only sold fifty copies.

Guinness World Records holds the record for being the book most often stolen from public libraries.

Lassie, the TV collie, first appeared in a 1930s short novel titled *Lassie Come Home*, written by Eric Mowbray Knight. The dog in the novel was based on Knight's real-life collie, Toots.

In 1898 (fourteen years prior to the *Titanic* tragedy), Morgan Robertson wrote a novel called *Futility*. The plot of the novel turned on the largest ship ever built hitting an iceberg in the Atlantic Ocean on a cold April night.

Keeping Warm with an Axe is the title of a real how-to book.

Mary Shelley wrote *Frankenstein* at the age of nineteen.

Virginia Woolf wrote all her books standing up.

At twelve years old, an African man named Ernest Loftus made his first entry in his diary and continued every day for ninety-one years.

People in Iceland read more books per capita than any other people in the world.

During the eighteenth century, books that were considered offensive were sometimes "punished" by being whipped.

The all-time bestselling electronic book is Stephen King's *Riding the Bullet*.

The only person to decline a Pulitzer Prize for Fiction was Sinclair Lewis for his book *Arrowsmith*.

Roger Ebert is the only film critic to have ever won the Pulitzer Prize.

Tom Sawyer was the first novel written on a typewriter.

Samuel Clemens, aka Mark Twain, smoked forty cigars a day for the last years of his life. He was born in 1835 when Halley's Comet appeared. He died in 1910 when Halley's Comet returned.

Ghosts appear in four Shakespearian plays: *Julius Caesar, Richard III, Hamlet,* and *Macbeth.*

> World heavyweight boxing champion Gene Tunney also lectured on Shakespeare at Yale University later in his life.

Shakespeare spelled his own name several different ways.

> Goethe couldn't stand the sound of barking dogs and could only write if he had an apple rotting in the drawer of his desk.

For the 66 percent of Americans who admit to reading in the bathroom, the preferred reading material is *Reader's Digest.*

> Ernest Vincent Wright wrote the fifty-thousand-word novel *Gatsby* without any word containing "e."

The original Aladdin story from *Tales of 1001 Arabian Nights* begins, "Aladdin was a little Chinese boy."

> Dr. Seuss pronounced his name so it would rhyme with *rejoice.* His birthday is March 2.

Dr. Seuss coined the word *nerd* in his 1950 book *If I Ran the Zoo.*

Sherlock Holmes's archenemy was Professor Moriarty. Holmes had a smarter brother named Mycroft.

Sherlock Holmes never said, "Elementary, my dear Watson."

Writer Edgar Allan Poe and LSD-advocate Timothy Leary were both kicked out of West Point.

Isaac Asimov is the only author to have a book in every Dewey decimal category.

Jacqueline Kennedy Onassis was the most famous editor at Doubleday & Co.

Hans Christian Anderson, author of many famous fairy tales, was word-blind. He never learned to spell correctly, and his publishers always found errors in his manuscripts.

Dr. Jekyll's first name is Henry.

Charles Dickens never finished his schooling. He was also an insomniac, who believed his best chance of sleeping was in the center of a bed facing directly north.

BIBLE TALK

Almost all the villains in the Bible have red hair.

The last word in the Bible is *Amen*.

The longest chapter in the Bible is Psalms 119.

There are more than 1,700 references to gems and precious stones in the King James Version of the Bible.

The Bible is the number-one shoplifted book in America.

The book of Esther in the Bible is the only book that does not mention the name of God.

The term *devil's advocate* comes from the Roman Catholic Church. When deciding if someone should be sainted, a devil's advocate is always appointed to give an alternative view.

The Bible has been translated into Klingon.

It is believed that Shakespeare was forty-six around the time the King James Version of the Bible was written. In Psalms 46, the forty-sixth word from the first word is *shake*, and the forty-sixth word from the last word is *spear*.

Every minute, forty-seven Bibles are sold or distributed throughout the world.

According to Genesis 1:20–22, the chicken came before the egg.

All Hebrew-originating names that end with the letters "el" have something to do with God.

A seventeenth-century Swedish philologist claimed that in the Garden of Eden God spoke Swedish, Adam spoke Danish, and the serpent spoke French.

ARE YOU AFRAID OF THE DARK?

A phonophobe fears noise.

Carcinomaphobia is the fear of cancer.

Paedophobia is a fear of children.

Nyctohylophobia is the fear of dark wooded areas, or forests at night.

Pyrophobia is the fear of fire.

Taphephobia is the fear of being buried alive.

Telephonophobia is the fear of telephones.

Papaphobia is the fear of popes.

Nycrophobia is the fear of darkness.

Lachanophobia is the fear of vegetables.

Entomophobia is the fear of insects.

Eosophobia is the fear of dawn.

Clinophobia is the fear of beds.

A gynaephobic man fears women.

Arnold Schonberg suffered from triskaidecphobia, the fear of the number thirteen. He died thirteen minutes from midnight on Friday the thirteenth.

Arachibutyrophobia is the fear of peanut butter sticking to the roof of your mouth.

Zoophobia is the fear of animals.

Tonsurphobia is the fear of haircuts.

Xenophobia is the fear of strangers or foreigners.

Phobatrivaphobia is fear of trivia about phobias.

NOW SAY IT THREE TIMES FAST

The world's longest name is Adolph Blaine Charles Daivid Earl Frederick Gerald Hubert Irvin John Kenneth Lloyd Martin Nero Oliver Paul Quincy Randolph Sherman Thomas Uncas Victor William Xerxes Yancy Zeus Wolfeschlegelsteinhausenbergerdorft Sr.

A hydrodaktulpsychicharmonica is a variety of musical glass.

Hydroxydesoxycorticosterone and hydroxydeoxycorticosterones are the largest anagrams.

The letters KGB stand for Komitet Gosudarstvennoy Bezopasnos.

The longest place name still in use is Taumatawhakatangihangaoauauotameteaturipukakapikimaungahoronukupokaiwhenuakitanatahu—a New Zealand hill.

The longest place name in Great Britain is that of a Welsh village: Gorsafawddachaidraigddanheddogleddollonpenrhynareurdraethceredigion.

The most difficult tongue-twister is "The sixth sick Sheik's sixth sheep's sick."

FORGET ME NOT

According to German legend, this flower gets its name from the last words of a knight, who was drowned while trying to pick some from the riverside for his lady.

IN THE BEGINNING

During early years of feudal rule in England, each shire had a reeve who was the law for that shire, called the shire reeve. When the term was taken to America, it was shortened to sheriff.

The phrase "rule of thumb" is derived from an old English law stating that you cannot beat your wife with anything wider than your thumb.

The phrase "sleep tight" originated when mattresses were set upon ropes woven through the bed frame. To remedy sagging ropes, one would use a bed key to tighten the rope.

The term *potty* comes from the pint-sized chamber pot built for children.

The word *noon* came from an old church term *none*, meaning "three." There was a monastic order that was so devout they declared they would not eat until that time.

Because they rang the bells indicating time, "none" came earlier and earlier. The townspeople called midday noon to ridicule them.

Before the turn of the century, newspapers were called tabloids, chronicles, gazettes, etc. Most had local stories, and far away stories were quite old because it took a while for stories to travel (and of course, they were subject to changes from hand to hand). With the advent of the teletype, stories could be broadcast all over at unheard-of speed. Several of the papers started carrying a section with stories from all over—north, east, west, and south—and that's why they are called *news*-papers.

Some coins used in the American colonies before the Revolutionary War were Spanish dollars, which could be cut into pieces, or bits. Because two pieces equaled one-quarter dollar, the expression "two bits" came into being as a name for twenty-five cents.

Ham radio operators coined the word *ham* from the expression "ham-fisted operators," a term used to describe early radio users who sent Morse code by pounding their fists.

"Happy as a clam" is from the expression "happy as a clam at high tide." Clams are only harvested when the tide is out.

The grand jury used to write *ignoramus* on the backs of indictments not found or not to be sent to court. This was often misconstrued as an indication of the stupidity of the jury, hence its present meaning.

In the 1940s, the Bich pen was changed to Bic for fear that Americans would pronounce it "bitch."

People didn't always say "hello" when they answered the phone. When the first regular phone service was established in 1878, people said "ahoy."

In the late nineteenth century and earlier years of the twentieth century, when gramophones or phonographs amplified the sound through large horns, woolen socks were often stuffed in them to cut down the noise; hence the phrase "put a sock in it."

The phrase "son of a gun" derives from the days when women were allowed to live on naval ships. The son of the gun was one born on the ship, often near the midship gun, behind a canvas screen. If the paternity was uncertain, the child was entered in the log as "son of a gun."

The magic word *abracadabra* was originally intended for the specific purpose of curing hay fever.

The phrase "Often a bridesmaid, but never a bride" actually comes from an advertisement for Listerine mouthwash.

The term *honeymoon* is derived from the Babylonians, who declared mead, a honey-flavored wine, the official wedding drink, stipulating that the bride's parents be required to keep the groom supplied with the drink for the month following the wedding.

The phrase "the boogeyman will get you" refers to the Boogey people who still inhabit an area of Indonesia. These people still act as pirates today and attack passing ships.

The term *mayday* used for signaling for help (after SOS) comes from the French *M'aidez*, which is pronounced *mayday* and means "help me."

"Three-dog night" (attributed to Australian Aborigines) came about because on especially cold nights, these nomadic people needed three dogs around them to keep from freezing.

In 1943, Navy officer Grace Hopper found a glitch in her computer. After investigating, she discovered the system had a bug—a real one. It turned out a moth had made its way into Hopper's computer. Though the word *bug* has meant "fault" or "defect" since as far back as the 1870s, Hopper's story is credited with making it the synonym of choice in the computer industry.

> Clans long ago who wanted to get rid of their unwanted people without killing them used to burn down their houses—hence the expression "get fired."

In Irish police stations in the nineteenth century—when public indecency was a serious crime—couples were charged with being Found Under Carnal Knowledge. Police abbreviated it to its initials and called it a F.U.C.K. charge.

> The expletive "Holy Toledo" refers to Toledo, Spain, which became an outstanding Christian cultural center in 1085.

The expression "What in tarnation?" comes from the original phrase "What in eternal damnation?"

> According to the *Encyclopedia Britannica, 11th Edition*, from 1910–1911, the word *toast* was borrowed from the Old French *toste*, which has the Latin root of *torrere, tostum*, meaning "to scorch or burn."

Crack gets its name because it crackles when you smoke it.

FOREIGN TRANSLATION

German is considered the sister language of English.

Amphibious is based on Greek words that mean living
a double life; amphibians live both on land and in water.

The word *rodent* comes from the Latin word *rodere*, meaning "to gnaw."

The words *assassination* and *bump* were invented by
Shakespeare.

The Old English word for sneeze is *fneosam*.

The *U* in U-boats stands for "underwater."

The word *constipation* comes from a Latin word that
means "to crowd together."

The word *curfew* originates from an old French word
that means "cover fire."

Corduroy comes from the French *cord du roi* or "cloth of
the king."

In French, *essay* means "to try, attempt."

The word *accordion* comes from the German word *akkord,* which means "agreement, harmony."

The word *calendar* comes from Latin and means "to call out."

The word *hangnail* comes from the Middle English: *ang-* ("painful") + *nail.* It has nothing to do with hanging.

The word *kangaroo* means "I don't know" in the language of Australian Aborigines. When Captain Cook approached natives of the Endeavor River tribe to ask what the strange animal he spotted was, he got "kangaroo" for an answer.

The word *cop* came from the English term "Constable on Patrol."

MAFIA is an acronym for Morte Alla Francia Italia Anela, or "Death to the French is Italy's Cry."

Mothers were originally named Mama or Mommy (in many languages) because they have mammary glands.

Influenza got its name from the fact that people believed the disease was because of the evil "influence" of stars.

THE NAKED TRUTH

A fable says that Truth and Falsehood went bathing; Falsehood came first out of the water and dressed herself in Truth's garments. Truth, unwilling to take those of Falsehood, went naked.

IN CASE YOU WERE WONDERING

A prestidigitator is another word for magician.

A castrated rooster is called a capon.

A conchologist studies mollusks and shells.

A deltiologist collects postcards.

A fingerprint is also known as a dactylogram.

A funambulist is a tightrope walker.

A horologist measures time.

A klazomaniac is someone who feels like shouting.

A librocubicularist is someone who reads in bed.

A phrenologist feels and interprets skull features.

A sultan's wife is called a sultana.

An anthropophagite eats people.

Killing a king is called regicide.

Spat-out food is called chanking.

The ball on top of a flagpole is called the truck.

A fox's tail is called a brush.

The two ends of a magnet are called poles.

The word *diastima* refers to having a gap between your teeth.

The word *lethologica* describes the state of not remembering the word you want to say.

The word *samba* means to rub navels together.

When your sink is full, the little hole that lets the water drain, instead of flowing over the side, is called a porcelator.

Women who wink at men are known as nictitating women.

A necropsy is an autopsy on animals.

A poem written to celebrate a wedding is called an epithalamium.

A scholar who studies the Marquis de Sade is called a Sadian, not a Sadist.

According to author Douglas Adams, a salween is the faint taste of dishwashing liquid in a cup of fresh tea.

Alma mater means "bountiful mother."

An animal epidemic is called an epizootic.

Degringolade means "to fall and disintegrate."

Dendrology is the study of trees.

Dibble means "to drink like a duck."

EEG stands for electroencephalogram.

EMI stands for electrical and musical instrument.

Groaking is to watch people eating in the hope that they will offer you some.

"Hara kiri" is an impolite way of saying the Japanese word *seppuku*, which means, literally, "belly splitting."

It is possible to drown and not die. Technically, the term *drowning* refers to the process of taking water into the lungs, not to death caused by that process.

Karaoke means "empty orchestra" in Japanese.

Kemosabe means "soggy shrub" in Navajo.

Koala is Aboriginal for "no drink."

Lead poisoning is known as plumbism.

Scatologists are experts who study feces.

Sekkusu means "sex" in Japanese.

Spain literally means "the land of rabbits."

The "You Are Here" arrow on a map is called the IDEO locator.

The third year of marriage is the leather anniversary.

The abbreviation "e.g." stands for *"exempli gratia,"* or "for example."

The abbreviation for pound, "lb.," comes from the astrological sign Libra, meaning "balance."

The French term *bourrage de crane* for wartime propaganda means "brain stuffing."

The infinity character on the keyboard is called a lemniscate.

The Japanese translation of *switch* is pronounced *suitchi.*

The name for fungal remains found in coal is sclerotinite.

The phrase "jet lag" was once called boat lag, back before airplanes existed.

The Sanskrit word for war means "desire for more cows."

The slang word *crap* comes from T. Crapper, the man who invented the modern toilet.

The slash character is called a virgule, or solidus. A URL uses slash characters, not backslash characters.

The word *karate* means "empty hand."

The word *byte* is a contraction of "by eight."

Trabant is the German word for "satellite."

Zorro means "fox" in Spanish.

A coward was originally a boy who took care of cows.

A group of officers is called a mess.

The next-to-last event is the penultimate, and the second-to-last is the antepenultimate.

The symbol on the pound key is called an anoctothorpe.

❧ SEMANTICS

Naked means "to be unprotected"; *nude* means "unclothed."

A hamlet is a village without a church, and a town is not a city until it has a cathedral.

FUN WITH LETTERS

Certain sounds in the English language are real germ spreaders, particularly the sounds *F, P, T, D,* and *S.*

Of all the words in the English language, the word *set* has the most definitions.

Rhythm and *syzygy* are the longest English words without vowels.

Skepticisms is the longest typed word that alternates hands.

The letter *J* does not appear anywhere on the periodic table of elements.

The letter *W* is the only letter in the alphabet that doesn't have one syllable; it has three.

The longest one-syllable word in the English language is *screeched*.

The longest word in the English language is 1,909 letters long, and it refers to a distinct part of DNA.

The most used letter in the English alphabet is *E*; *Q* is the least used.

The oldest word in the English language is *town*.

The only fifteen-letter word that can be spelled without repeating a letter is *uncopyrightable*.

The only contemporary words that end with -*gry* are *angry* and *hungry*.

The words *racecar* and *kayak* are palindromes; they're the same whether they are read left to right or right to left.

Only four words in the English language end in -*dous*: *tremendous*, *horrendous*, *stupendous*, and *hazardous*.

Only three world capitals begin with the letter *O* in English: Ottawa, Canada; Oslo, Norway; and Ouagadougou, Burkina Faso.

Six words in the English language have the letter combination *uu*: muumuu, vacuum, continuum, duumvirate, duumvir, and residuum.

Ten body parts are only three letters long: eye, ear, leg, arm, jaw, gum, toe, lip, hip, and rib.

There was no punctuation until the fifteenth century.

When two words are combined to form a single word (e.g., motor + hotel = motel; breakfast + lunch = brunch), the new word is called a portmanteau.

You would have to count to one thousand to use the letter *A* in the English language to spell a whole number.

Bookkeeper is the only word in the English language with three consecutive double letters.

Facetious and *abstemious* contain all the vowels in the correct order, as does *arsenious*, meaning "containing arsenic."

Cleveland spelled backward is *DNA level C*.

There are only twelve letters in the Hawaiian alphabet. Hawaiian words do not contain consonant clusters. For example, Kahlúa is not a Hawaiian word.

"I am" is the shortest complete sentence in the English language.

In England in the 1880s, *pants* was considered a dirty word.

In English, four is the only number that has the same number of letters as its value.

Stewardesses is the longest word that is typed with only the left hand.

No word in the English language rhymes with month, orange, silver, or purple.

Quisling is the only word in the English language to start with "quis."

Maine is the only state whose name is just one syllable.

The most recent year that could be written upside down and right side up and appear the same was 1961. The next year this will be possible will be 6009.

LANGUAGE BARRIER

There are about five thousand different languages spoken on Earth.

Chevrolet tried marketing a Chevrolet Nova in Spanish-speaking countries—it didn't sell well because *"no va"* means "doesn't go" in Spanish.

In Italy, a campaign for Schweppes Tonic Water translated the name into Schweppes Toilet Water.

In Papua New Guinea, there are villages within five miles of each other that speak different languages.

More than twenty-six dialects of Quichua are spoken in Ecuador.

Native speakers of Japanese learn Spanish more easily than English. Native speakers of English learn Spanish more easily than Japanese.

Polish is the only word in the English language that, when capitalized, is changed from a noun or a verb to a nationality.

Rio de Janeiro translates to River of January.

The correct response to the Irish greeting "Top of the morning to you" is, "And the rest of the day to yourself."

The *D* in D-day stands for "day." The French term for D-day is *J-jour.*

The Kentucky Fried Chicken slogan "Finger-lickin' good" came out as "Eat your fingers off" in Chinese.

The three best-known western names in China are Jesus Christ, Richard Nixon, and Elvis Presley.

The stress in Hungarian words always falls on the first syllable.

No Spanish words begin with the letter *W* (except for those of American-English origin).

The Eskimo language has more than twenty words to describe different kinds of snow.

WAS IT AT CHUCK E. CHEESE?

The earliest document in Latin in a woman's handwriting is an invitation to a birthday party from the first century C.E.

SPECIAL OCCASIONS

World Tourist Day is observed on September 27.

October 10 is National Metric Day.

November 19 is Have a Bad Day Day.

November 29 is National Sinky Day, a day to eat over one's sink and worship it.

COMMON THREADS

The most common name for a goldfish is Jaws.

The most common name in Italy is Mario Rossi.

The most common name in the world is Mohammed.

The most common Spanish surname is Garcia.

The most common Russian surname is Ivanov.

The most common Swedish surname is Johansson.

The most common name for a boat in 1996 was *Serenity*.

ON THE MENU

WATER WORLD

Drinking water after eating reduces the acid in your mouth by 61 percent.

Forty-eight million people in the United States receive their drinking water from private or household wells.

In the typical Canadian home, 45 percent of water is used for the toilet, 28 percent is used for bathing and personal matters, 23 percent is used for laundry or dishes, and 4 percent is used for cooking or drinking purposes.

It's impossible to get water out of a rimless tire.

Less than 2 percent of the water on Earth is fresh.

A tea in China called white tea is simply boiled water.

THE HOUSE THAT RONALD BUILT

Ray Kroc bought McDonald's for $2.7 million in 1961 from the McDonald brothers.

Seven percent of Americans eat McDonald's every day.

Four hundred quarter-pounders can be made out of one cow.

A man named Ed Peterson is the inventor of the Egg McMuffin.

The big *M* on McDonald's signs in Paris is the only one in the world that is white, rather than yellow; it was thought that yellow was too tacky.

McDonald's in New Zealand serves apricot pies instead of cherry ones.

The McDonald's at The Skydome in Toronto is the only one in the world that sells hot dogs.

On average, there are 178 sesame seeds on each McDonald's Big Mac bun.

SODA OR POP?

Carbonated water, with nothing else in it, can dissolve limestone, talc, and many other low-Mohs hardness minerals. Coincidentally, carbonated water is the main ingredient in soda pop.

The citrus soda 7-Up was created in 1929; "7" was selected because the original containers were seven ounces. "Up" indicated the direction of the bubbles.

Fanta Orange is the third largest selling soft drink in the world.

Coca-Cola was first served at Jacob's Pharmacy in Atlanta in 1886 for only five cents a glass. The formula for Coca-Cola was created by pharmacist John Pemberton. Only two people in the world know the secret recipe for Coca-Cola.

Earl Dean developed the bottle design for Coca-Cola.

Coca-Cola was originally green.

A can of Diet Coke will float in water, while a can of regular Coke sinks.

Coca-Cola owns the world's second largest truck fleet.

Coke is used to clean up blood spills on highways.

Diet Coke was only invented in 1983.

Pepsi originally contained pepsin, hence the name.

The first western consumer product sold in the former Soviet Union was Pepsi Cola.

In 1989, Pepsi came out with a morning soft drink called Pepsi AM. It didn't last long on the market.

Pepsi is commonly used by wooden boat owners to clean mold from decks. You can spill it on for about thirty seconds, but it needs to be rinsed to be sure it does not erode the decks completely.

HOLD YOUR LIQUOR

A full 7 percent of the entire Irish barley crop goes to the production of Guinness beer.

Beer foam will go down if you lick your finger and then stick it in the beer.

Researchers in Denmark found that beer tastes best when drunk to the accompaniment of a certain musical tone. The optimal frequency is different for each beer, they reported. The correct harmonious tone for Carlsberg lager, for example, is 510 to 520 cycles per second.

Widows of a recently deceased king among the Baganda people of Uganda have the honor of drinking the beer in which the king's entrails have been cleaned.

The Bloody Mary is known as the "Queen of Drinks" and was invented in Harry's Bar in Paris in the 1930s.

If you put a raisin in a glass of champagne, it will keep floating to the top and sinking to the bottom.

The first man to distill bourbon whiskey was a Baptist preacher in 1789.

Wine will spoil if exposed to light, hence the tinted bottles.

Lab tests can detect traces of alcohol in urine six to twelve hours after a person has stopped drinking.

In medieval England, beer was often served with breakfast.

Vikings used the skulls of their enemies as drinking vessels.

CRACKING SOME NUTS

Almonds are a member of the peach family. They are the oldest, most widely cultivated and extensively used nuts in the world.

Peanuts are cholesterol-free. They are one of the ingredients of dynamite.

George Washington Carver invented peanut butter. It takes more than five hundred peanuts to make one twelve-ounce jar of peanut butter.

Australian chemist John Macadamia discovered the macadamia nut.

The only real food U.S. astronauts are allowed in space are pecan nuts.

In the summer, walnuts get a tan.

EAT YOUR VEGGIES

Vegetarians make up 4 percent of the U.S. population.

Ninety percent of the vitamin C in brussels sprouts is lost in cooking.

You use more calories eating celery than there are in celery itself.

Eggplant is a member of the thistle family.

Eating raw onions is good for unblocking a stuffed nose.

Onions are low in calories and a good source of vitamin C, calcium, potassium, and fiber. They also help circulation.

Onions get their distinctive smell by soaking up sulfur from the soil.

The oldest known vegetable is the pea.

The most popular sweet pepper is the bell pepper.

The heat of peppers is rated on the Scoville scale.

The color of a chili is no indication of its spiciness, but size usually is—the smaller the pepper, the hotter it is.

Pumpkins contain vitamin A and potassium.

Turnips turn green when sunburned.

TUTTI FRUITY

Pomology is the study of fruit.

Tomatoes and cucumbers are fruits.

Apples, not caffeine, are more efficient for waking you up in the morning.

Fresh apples float because 25 percent of their volume is air.

The avocado has the most calories of any fruit.

The most widely eaten fruit in America is the banana.

The average banana weighs 126 grams.

Approximately seventeen thousand bananas are eaten each week in the Boston University dining room.

Bananas do not grow on trees but on rhizomes.

Cranberries are sorted for ripeness by bouncing them; a fully ripened cranberry can be dribbled like a basketball.

Cranberry jelly is the only jelly flavor that comes from the real fruit, not artificial flavoring.

A cucumber consists of 96 percent water.

Grapes explode when you put them in the microwave.

Lemons contain more sugar than strawberries.

Seeds are missing from a navel orange. The bigger the navel, the sweeter the orange.

In Ivrea, Italy, thousands of citizens celebrate the beginning of Lent by throwing oranges at one another.

Orange juice helps the body absorb iron easily when consumed with a meal.

The most common pear worldwide is the Bartlett. It is bell shaped, sweet, and soft, with a light green color.

More than a third of all pineapples come from Hawaii.

Pineapples do not ripen after they have been picked.

Tomatina is the legendary Spanish tomato-throwing festival.

More than two hundred varieties of watermelon are grown in the United States.

JAVA TIME

Coffee is the world's most popular stimulant. It is the second largest item of international commerce in the world.

When a coffee seed is planted, it takes five years to yield consumable fruit.

There are more than one hundred chemicals in one cup of coffee.

Coffee does not help sober up a drunk person. In many cases, it may actually increase the adverse effects of alcohol.

Too much caffeine can cause heart palpitations.

A Saudi Arabian woman can get a divorce if her husband doesn't give her coffee.

In Turkey in the sixteenth and seventeenth centuries, anyone caught drinking coffee was put to death.

YOU SAY TOMATO, I SAY AVOCADO

A chili pepper isn't a pepper. In fact, more than two hundred kinds of chili peppers aren't peppers.

There is no such thing as blue food—even blueberries are purple.

THE SWEET SPOT

M&Ms stands for the last names of Forrest Mars Sr., the sweet maker, and his associate, Bruce Murrie. The candy was developed so soldiers could eat sweets without getting their fingers sticky.

There are more brown M&Ms in plain M&Ms than in peanut M&Ms.

The top layer of a wedding cake, known as the groom's cake, is usually a fruit cake so it will last until the couple's first anniversary, when they will eat it.

As much as fifty gallons of maple sap are used to make a single gallon of maple sugar.

There are more doughnut shops per capita in Canada than in any other country.

Pound cake is so called because the original recipe required one pound of butter.

The only food that does not spoil is honey. It is used as a center for golf balls and in antifreeze mixtures.

When honey is swallowed, it enters the blood stream within a period of twenty minutes.

The most popular ice cream flavor is vanilla.

Ice cream was originally made without sugar and eggs. Seaweed is one of the ingredients in some ice cream.

Five jelly flavors that flopped: celery, coffee, cola, apple, and chocolate.

Less than 3 percent of Nestlé's sales are for chocolate.

Eleanor Roosevelt ate three chocolate-covered garlic balls every day for most of her adult life.

Eating chocolate was once considered a temptation of the devil.

 NO WONDER WE'RE FAT

During your lifetime, you will eat sixty thousand pounds of food—the weight of six elephants.

The average American chews 190 sticks of gum, drinks 600 sodas and 800 gallons of water, and eats 135 pounds of sugar and 19 pounds of cereal per year.

The biggest-selling restaurant food is french fries.

The estimated number of M&Ms sold each day in the United States is two hundred million.

The amount of potato chips Americans eat each year weighs six times more than the *Titanic*.

A can of SPAM is opened every four seconds.

Americans on average eat eighteen acres of pizza every day. Saturday night is the biggest night of the week for eating pizza.

Dunkin' Donuts serves about 112,500 doughnuts each day.

More popcorn is sold in Dallas than anywhere else in the United States.

Two million different combinations of sandwiches can be created from a Subway menu.

GREAT MOMENTS IN
GASTRONOMIC HISTORY

The food of the Greek gods was called ambrosia.

The chocolate-chip cookie was invented in 1933.

Blueberry Jelly Bellies were created especially for Ronald Reagan.

California's Frank Epperson invented the Popsicle in 1905, when he was eleven years old.

Chefs started using onions five thousand years ago to spice up their cooking.

Doughnuts originated in Holland.

Dry cereal for breakfast was invented by John Henry Kellogg at the turn of the twentieth century.

In 1983, a Japanese artist made a copy of the *Mona Lisa* completely out of toast.

Fortune cookies were actually invented in America by Charles Jung in 1918.

Jelly Belly jelly beans were the first jelly beans in outer space when they went up with astronauts in the June 21, 1983, voyage of the space shuttle *Challenger*.

🌰 WE'D LOVE TO HAVE YOU FOR DINNER . . .

Sawney Beane, his wife, eight sons, six daughters, and thirty-two grandchildren were a family of cannibals who lived in the caves near Galloway, Scotland, in the early seventeenth century. Although the total number is not known, it is believed they claimed more than fifty victims per year. The entire family was taken by an army detachment to Edinburgh and executed, apparently without trial.

British politician John Montagu, the 46th Earl of Sandwich, is credited with naming the sandwich. He developed the habit of eating beef between slices of toast so he could continue playing cards uninterrupted.

Ketchup originated in China.

Laws forbidding the sale of sodas on Sunday prompted William Garwood to invent the ice-cream sundae in Evanston, Illinois, in 1875.

Potato chips were invented in Louisiana in 1853.

Potatoes were first imported by Europe in the 1500s on Spanish ships returning from Peru.

Beijing boasts the world's largest Kentucky Fried Chicken restaurant.

Almost 425,000 hot dogs and buns and 160,000 hamburgers and cheeseburgers were served at Woodstock '99.

The English word *soup* comes from the Middle Ages word *sop*, which means a slice of bread over which roast drippings were poured.

COUNTERINTUITIVE BUT TRUE

Vanilla is used to make chocolate.

RECORD BREAKERS

The highest lifetime yield of milk for a single cow is 55,849 gallons.

The hottest chili in the world is the habanero.

The largest apple pie ever baked was forty feet by twenty-three feet.

The largest hamburger in the world weighed in at 5,520 pounds.

The largest ketchup bottle is a 170-foot water tower.

INTERNATIONAL PALETTES

Dinner guests during the medieval times in England were expected to bring their own knives to the table.

In eighteenth-century France, visitors to the royal palace in Versailles were allowed to stand in a roped-off section of the main dining room and watch the king and queen eat.

In certain parts of India and ancient China, mouse meat was considered a delicacy.

Each year, Americans spend more on cat food than on baby food.

It is estimated that Americans consume ten million tons of turkey on Thanksgiving Day. Due to turkey's high sulfur content, Americans also produce enough gas to fly a fleet of seventy-five *Hindenburgs* from Los Angeles to New York in twenty-four hours.

The Southern dish "chitlins" is made up of pigs' small intestines.

Yogurt intake among North Americans has quadrupled in the past twenty years.

In Australia, the number-one topping for pizza is eggs. In Chile, the favorite topping is mussels and clams. In the United States, it's pepperoni.

The world's number-one producer and consumer of fresh pork is China.

China produces 278,564,356,980 eggs per year.

China's Beijing Duck Restaurant can seat nine thousand people at one time.

If China imported just 10 percent of its rice needs, the price on the world market would increase by 80 percent.

France has the highest per capita consumption of cheese. More than half of the different types of cheese in the world come from France.

The glue on Israeli postage stamps is certified kosher.

Japan is the largest exporter of frogs' legs.

A company in Taiwan makes dinnerware out of wheat, so you can eat your plate.

CULINARY ER

Astronauts are not allowed to eat beans before they go into space because passing wind in a space suit damages it.

Since 1978, at least thirty-seven people have died as a result of shaking vending machines in an attempt to get free merchandise. More than one hundred have been injured.

Some people drink the urine of pregnant women to build up their immune systems.

The liquid inside young coconuts can be used as a substitute for blood plasma in an emergency.

You should not eat a crayfish with a straight tail. It was dead before it was cooked.

Nutmeg is extremely poisonous if injected intra-venously.

Chewing gum while peeling onions will keep you from crying.

A LITTLE BIT GRAINY

There are more than fifteen thousand different kinds of rice. Rice is grown on more than 10 percent of the earth's farmable surface and is the main food for half of the people of the world.

Rice is thrown at weddings as a symbol of fertility.

Shredded Wheat was the first ready-to-eat breakfast cereal.

The wheat that produces a one-pound loaf of bread requires two tons of water to grow.

No two cornflakes look the same.

SO THAT'S WHERE OUR
TAX DOLLARS GO

The U.S. government spent $277,000 on "pickle research" in 1993.

NO, I SAID CONDIMENTS

Salt is the only rock humans can eat. Only 5 percent of salt produced ends up on the dinner table. The rest is used for packing meat; building roads; feeding livestock; tanning leather; and manufacturing glass, soap, ash, and washing compounds.

Salt is one of the few spices that is all taste and no smell.

Table salt is the only commodity that hasn't risen dramatically in price in the last one hundred fifty years.

Tabasco sauce is made by fermenting vinegar and hot peppers in a French oak barrel that has three inches of salt on top and is aged for three years until all the salt is diffused through the barrel.

Worcestershire sauce is basically anchovy ketchup.

The number 57 on a Heinz ketchup bottle represents the number of varieties of pickle the company once had.

THINGS THAT MAKE YOU GO "MOOO . . ."

Pound for pound, hamburgers cost more than new cars.

Reindeer's milk has more fat than cow's milk.

Sheep's milk is used to produce Roquefort cheese.

The fat molecules in goat's milk are five times smaller than those found in cow's milk.

AROUND THE HOUSE

DEUCES ARE WILD

Each king in a deck of playing cards represents a great king from history: spades—King David, clubs—Alexander the Great, hearts—Charlemagne, and diamonds—Julius Caesar.

Each of the suits in a deck of cards represents the four major pillars of the economy in the Middle Ages: hearts represented the Church, spades represented the military, clubs represented agriculture, and diamonds represented the merchant class.

In every deck of cards, the King of Hearts is sticking his sword through his head. That's why he's often called the Suicide King.

For a deck of cards to be mixed up enough to play with properly, it should be shuffled at least seven times.

Playing cards became the first paper currency of Canada in 1685, when the French governor used them to pay off some war debts.

Playing cards in India are round.

The Nine of Hearts playing card is considered the symbol of love.

The Ace of Spades playing card symbolizes death.

COMMON CENTS

The ridges on the sides of coins are called reeding or milling. A dime has 118 ridges around the edge. A quarter has 119 ridges.

How valuable is the penny you found lying on the ground? If it takes just a second to pick it up, a person could make $36 per hour just picking up pennies.

It's rumored that sucking on a copper penny will cause a Breathalyzer to read zero.

On the new U.S. $100 bill, the time on the clock tower of Independence Hall is 4:10.

The Australian $5, $10, $20, $50, and $100 notes are made of plastic.

The face of a penny can hold thirty drops of water.

The first U.S. coin to bear the words "United States of America" was a penny made in 1727. It was also inscribed with the plain-spoken motto, "Mind your own business."

The original fifty-cent piece in Australian decimal currency had around $100 worth of silver in it before it was replaced with a less-expensive twelve-sided coin.

At the height of inflation in Germany in the early 1920s, approximately two dollars were equal to a quintillion German marks.

KISSABLY FRESH

Colgate faced a big obstacle marketing toothpaste in Spanish-speaking countries. *Colgate* translates into the command "go hang yourself."

More people use blue toothbrushes than red ones.

Oral-B is a combination of "oral hygiene" and the letter B, which stands for the word *better*.

Some toothpaste contains antifreeze.

Dentists recommended that a toothbrush be kept six feet away from a toilet to avoid airborne particles resulting from the flush.

Americans spend $1.5 billion every year on toothpaste.

JUST A SCRATCH

Four thousand people are injured by teapots every year.

A toothpick is the object most often choked on by Americans. Every year, more than 8,800 people injure themselves in some way with a toothpick.

On average, one hundred people choke on ballpoint pens every year.

Forty thousand Americans are injured by toilets every year.

In 1981, a man had a heart attack after playing the game *Berserk*—video gaming's only known fatality.

In 1990, there were about fifteen thousand vacuum cleaner–related accidents in the United States.

THE ROYAL THRONE

A flush toilet exists today that dates back to 2000 B.C.E.

About a third of people flush while they are still sitting on the toilet.

Alaska has more outhouses than any other state.

In 1825, the first toilet was installed in the White House.

In true kingly fashion, Elvis passed away while sitting on the throne.

Most toilets flush in E flat.

Poet Henry Wadsworth Longfellow was the first American to have plumbing installed in his house, in 1840.

The first toilet ever seen on television was on *Leave It to Beaver*.

The Soviet Sukhoi-34 is the first strike fighter with a toilet in it.

Toilets in Australia flush counterclockwise.

SIMPLY SARTORIAL

Bill Bowerman, founder of Nike, got his first shoe idea after staring at a waffle iron. He got the idea of using squared spikes to make shoes lighter.

The plastic things on the end of shoelaces are called aglets.

If you lace your shoes from the inside to the outside, the fit will be snugger around your big toe.

North Americans spend almost $18 billion on footwear a year.

Jeans were named after Genoa, Italy, where the first denim cloth was made.

The YKK on the zipper of your Levi's stands for Yoshida Kogyo Kabushibibaisha, the world's largest zipper manufacturer.

Neckties were first worn in Croatia. That's why they were called cravats (*cro-vats*).

Most people button their shirts upward.

The armhole in clothing is called an armsaye.

The bra Marilyn Monroe wore in the movie *Some Like It Hot* was sold for $14,000.

In 1955, one-third of all watches sold were Timexes.

The quartz crystal in your wristwatch vibrates 32,768 times a second.

TOYING AROUND

Since the Lego Group began manufacturing blocks in 1949, more than 189 billion pieces in 2,000 different shapes have been produced. This is enough for about thirty Lego pieces for every living person on Earth. Five-thousandths of a millimeter is the tolerance of accuracy at the Lego mold factories.

Ninety-four percent of all households in Belgium with children under the age of fourteen years old own Lego products.

Barbie's full name is Barbara Millicent Roberts. Barbie's measurements if she were life-size would be 5 feet, 9 inches tall, 33-18-31½.

There are more Barbie dolls in Italy than there are Canadians in Canada.

Totally Hair Barbie is the best-selling Barbie of all time.

Slinkys were invented by an airplane mechanic; he was playing with engine parts and realized the possible secondary use of one of the springs.

The Slinky is sold on every continent of the world except Antarctica. If you took a standard Slinky and stretched it out, it would measure eighty-seven feet.

In 1946, the first TV toy commercial aired. It was for Mr. Potato Head.

In 1980, Namco released Pac-Man, the most popular video game (or arcade game) of all time. The original name was going to be Puck Man, but executives saw the potential for vandals to scratch out part of the *P* in the game's marquee and labeling.

It takes an average of 48 to 100 tries to solve a Rubik's Cube puzzle. If done perfectly, any Rubik's Cube combination can be solved in seventeen turns.

The hula hoop was the biggest-selling toy in 1957.

The yo-yo originated in the Philippines, where it is used as a weapon in hunting.

When the divorce rate goes up in the United States, toy makers say the sale of toys also rises.

The hundred billionth crayon made by Crayola was Periwinkle Blue.

In the 1985 Boise, Idaho, mayoral election, there were four write-in votes for Mr. Potato Head.

WHAT DO YOU MEAN?

Camera shutter speed B stands for "bulb."

Mosquito repellants do not repel. They hide you. The spray blocks the mosquito's sensors so they do not know you are there.

Scotchgard is a combination of the words *Scotch*, meaning "Scotsman," and a misspelling of *guard*, meaning "to protect."

The holes in flyswatters are used to lower air resistance.

Scotch tape has been used as an anti-corrosive shield on the *Goodyear Blimp*.

The Ramses brand condom is named after the great Pharaoh Ramses II, who fathered more than 160 children.

HAMMER TIME

The side of a hammer is called a cheek.

The end of a hammer, opposite the striking end, is called a peen.

THE IVORY TOWER

Ivory bar soap floating was the result of a mistake. The manufacturer had been mixing the soap formula and causing excess air bubbles that made it float. Customers wrote and told them how much they loved that it floated, and it has floated ever since.

Approximately thirty billion cakes of Ivory Soap had been manufactured by 1990.

FEELING A BIT AVERAGE

The average person looks at eight houses before buying one.

The average lead pencil can draw a line thirty-five miles long or write approximately fifty thousand English words.

The average mouse pad is 8.75 inches by 7.5 inches.

The average woman consumes six pounds of lipstick in her lifetime.

The average woman's handbag weighs three to five pounds.

ALTERNATIVE FUNCTIONS

Ketchup is excellent for cleaning brass, especially tarnished or corroded brass.

Kleenex tissues were originally used as filters in gas masks.

Mixing Sani-Flush and Comet cleaners has been known to cause explosions.

People in China sometimes use firecrackers around their homes as fire alarms.

DISHING THE DIRT

Each of us generates five pounds of garbage a day; most of it is paper.

It takes a plastic container fifty thousand years to start decomposing.

According to a market research survey, 68 percent of consumers who receive junk mail actually open the envelopes.

MEASURING UP

A 60-minute cassette contains 565 feet of tape.

The diameter of the wire in a standard paper clip is 1 millimeter, or about 0.04 inches.

Aluminum is strong enough to support ninety thousand pounds per square inch.

KEEPING YOUR COOL

Rubber bands last longer when refrigerated.

Some Eskimos have been known to use refrigerators to keep their food from freezing.

HOME DÉCOR

A good-quality Persian rug, which contains one million knots in every three square inches, can last as long as five hundred years.

A typical double mattress contains as many as two million house dust mites.

HISTORY'S MYSTERIES

HOW DO YOU PLEAD?

A Virginia law requires all bathtubs to be kept out in the yard, not inside the house.

According to a British law passed in 1845, attempting to commit suicide was a capital offense. Offenders could be hanged for trying.

Celebrating Christmas was once illegal in England.

Dueling is legal in Paraguay as long as both parties are registered blood donors.

Impotence is legal grounds for divorce in twenty-four American states.

In a tradition dating back to the beginning of the Westminster system of government, the bench in the middle of a Westminster parliament is two-and-a-half sword lengths long. This was so the government and opposition couldn't have a go at each other if it all got a bit heated.

In Alaska, it is illegal to shoot at a moose from the window of an airplane or other flying vehicle.

In Athens, Greece, a driver's license can be taken away by law if the driver is deemed either "unbathed" or "poorly dressed."

In Baltimore, it is illegal to wash or scrub a sink, regardless of how dirty it is.

In Cleveland, Ohio, it is illegal to catch mice without a hunting license.

In England during Queen Victoria's reign, it was illegal to be a homosexual but not a lesbian, the reason being that when the queen was approving the law, she wouldn't believe that women would do that.

In Hartford, Connecticut, it is illegal for a husband to kiss his wife on Sundays.

In Helsinki, Finland, instead of giving parking tickets, the police usually deflate tires.

In Italy, it is illegal to make coffins out of anything except nutshells or wood.

In Jasmine, Saskatchewan, it is illegal for a cow to moo within three hundred kilometers of a private home.

In Kentucky, it is illegal to carry ice cream in your back pocket.

In Sweden, although prostitution is legal, it is illegal for anyone to use the services of a prostitute.

In Texas, it is illegal to put graffiti on someone else's cow.

In the United Kingdom, there is no Act of Parliament making it illegal to commit murder. Murder is only illegal due to legal precedent.

It is against the law to stare at the mayor of Paris.

In Singapore, it is against the law to urinate in an elevator.

In Sweden, it is illegal to train a seal to balance a ball on its nose.

In California, it is illegal to eat oranges while bathing.

In Bladworth, Saskatchewan, it is illegal to frown at cows.

It is illegal to grow or sell pork in Israel.

In Arizona, it is illegal to hunt camels.

In Malaysia, it is illegal for restaurants to substitute toilet paper as table napkins. Repeat offenders go to jail.

It used to be law in France that children's names had to be taken from an official government list.

In Iceland, it was once against the law to have a pet dog in a city.

In one city in Switzerland, it was once against the law to slam your car door.

Mailing an entire building has been illegal in the United States since 1916, when a man mailed a forty-thousand-ton brick house across Utah to avoid high freight rates.

Pennsylvania was the first colony to legalize witchcraft.

A monkey was once tried and convicted for smoking a cigarette in South Bend, Indiana.

According to the United States Refuse Act of 1899, every industrial discharge into bodies of water since 1899 has been a crime.

Every citizen of Kentucky is required by law to take a bath at least once a year.

If you live in Michigan, it is illegal to put a skunk in your boss's desk.

In Hartford, Connecticut, you may not, under any circumstances, cross the street walking on your hands.

In Idaho, a citizen is forbidden by law to give another citizen a box of candy that weighs more than fifty pounds.

In Indiana, it is illegal to ride public transportation for at least thirty minutes after eating garlic.

In Minnesota, it is illegal for women to be dressed up as Santa Claus on city streets.

In Morrisville, Pennsylvania, women need a legal permit before they can wear lipstick in public.

In some parts of Alabama, it is illegal to carry a comb in your pocket.

In the Rhode Island legislature during the 1970s, it was proposed that there be a tax of $2 on every act of sexual intercourse.

In Oklahoma, it is against the law to hunt whale.

It is illegal for boys in ninth grade to grow a mustache in Binghamton, New York.

In Omaha, Nebraska, it's against the law to burp or sneeze in a church.

In Kansas, it's against the law to catch fish with your bare hands.

It's against the law to ride down the streets of Brewton, Alabama, in a motorboat.

Most burglaries occur in the winter.

The state legislature in North Dakota has rejected a proposal to erect signs specifically warning motorists not to throw human waste on to the roadside. Maintenance workers report at least twenty incidents of road crews being sprayed with urine after rupturing urine-filled plastic bottles that became swollen in the hot sun. Opponents of the measure say they're afraid the signs would discourage tourism.

Under the law of Mississippi, there's no such thing as a female Peeping Tom.

✏ THAT'S WHAT WE CALL A MILESTONE

In 1976, a Los Angeles secretary named Jannene Swift officially married a fifty-pound rock. The ceremony was witnessed by more than twenty people.

ANCIENT CIVILIZATIONS

Ancient Sybarites taught their horses to dance to music to make their parades more glamorous.

Ancient Sumerians thought the liver made blood and the heart was the center of thought.

The ancient Etruscans painted women white and men red in the wall paintings they used to decorate tombs.

Abdul Kassam Ismael, Grand Vizier of Persia in the tenth century, carried his library with him wherever he went. The 117,000 volumes were carried by 400 camels trained to walk in alphabetical order.

At the turn of the previous millennium, Dublin had the largest slave market in the world, run by the Vikings.

A two-hundred-year-old piece of Tibetan cheese was auctioned off for $1,513 in 1993.

Aztec emperor Montezuma had a nephew, Cuitlahac, whose name meant "plenty of excrement."

In 1281, the Mongol army of Kublai Khan tried to invade Japan but was ravaged by a hurricane that destroyed their fleet.

The Toltecs, seventh-century native Mexicans, went to battle with wooden swords so as not to kill their enemies.

There was a pony express in Persia many centuries before Christ. Riders on this ancient circuit, wearing special colored headbands, delivered the mail across the vast stretch of Asia Minor, sometimes riding for hundreds of miles without a break.

In ancient Japan, public contests were held to see who in a town could break wind loudest and longest. Winners were awarded many prizes and received great acclaim.

UNRECORDED HISTORY

During the Cambrian period, about five hundred million years ago, a day was only 20.6 hours long.

The name of the asteroid that was believed to have killed the dinosaurs was Chixalub (pronounced *sheesh-uh-loob*).

WALK LIKE AN EGYPTIAN

Ra was the sun god of ancient Egypt.

In ancient Egypt, the apricot was called the egg of the sun, killing a cat was a crime punishable by death, and Egyptians paid their taxes in honey.

Ancient Egyptians shaved off their eyebrows to mourn the death of their cats.

Ancient Egyptians slept on pillows made of stone.

About three hundred years ago, most Egyptians died by the time they were thirty.

According to the Greek historian Herodotus, Egyptian men never became bald. The reason for this, Herodotus claimed, was that as children, Egyptian males had their heads shaved, and their scalps were continually exposed to the health-giving rays of the sun. In Egypt around 1500 B.C.E., a shaved head was considered the ultimate in feminine beauty. Egyptian women removed every hair from their heads with special gold tweezers and polished their scalps to a high sheen with buffing cloths.

If a surgeon in ancient Egypt lost a patient while performing an operation, his hands were cut off.

Pharaoh Ramses II died in 1225 B.C.E. At the time of his death, he had fathered 111 sons and 67 daughters.

The Egyptian city of Alexandria was discovered by Alexander the Great in 331 B.C.E.

The Egyptian hieroglyph for one hundred thousand is a tadpole.

The first known contraceptive was crocodile dung, used by Egyptians in 2000 B.C.E.

Cleopatra married two of her brothers.

Preparing an Egyptian mummy sometimes took up to seventy days. Dead Egyptian noblewomen were given the special treatment of being allowed a few days to ripen so the embalmers wouldn't find them too attractive.

On some mummies that have been unwrapped, the total length of the bandages has been about 1.5 miles.

Tomb robbers believed that knocking off Egyptian sarcophagi's noses would stall curses.

A golden razor removed from King Tut's tomb was still sharp enough to be used.

IT'S GREEK TO ME

The ruins of Troy are located in Turkey.

In 290 B.C.E., Aristarchus was the first Greek astronomer to suggest that the sun was the center of the solar system.

At the height of its power, in 400 B.C.E., the Greek city of Sparta had twenty-five thousand citizens and five hundred thousand slaves.

In ancient Greece, women counted their age from the date they were married.

ROMAN HOLIDAY

High-wire acts have been enjoyed since the time of the ancient Greeks and Romans. Antique medals have been excavated from Greek islands depicting men ascending inclined cords and walking across ropes stretched between cliffs. The Greeks called these high-wire performers neurobates or oribates. In the Roman city of Herculaneum, there is a fresco representing an aerialist high on a rope, dancing and playing a flute. Sometimes Roman tightrope walkers stretched cables between the tops of two neighboring hills and performed comic dances and pantomimes while crossing.

Trivia is the Roman goddess of sorcery, hounds, and the crossroads.

After the great fire of Rome in 64 C.E., the emperor Nero ostensibly decided to lay the blame on Christians residing in the city of Rome. He gathered them together, crucified them, covered them in pitch, and burned them. He walked around his gardens admiring the view.

Ancient Romans believed that birds mated on February 14.

Flamingo tongues were a common delicacy at Roman feasts.

Hannibal had only one eye after losing the other to a disease he caught while attacking Rome.

In ancient Rome, it was considered a sign of leadership to be born with a crooked nose.

In ancient Rome, weasels were used to catch mice.

It was decreed by law in the Roman Empire that all young maidens be fed rabbit meat because it would make them more beautiful and more willing.

> Julius Caesar tried to beef up the population of Rome by offering rewards to couples who had many children.

Spartacus led the revolt of the Roman slaves and gladiators in 73 C.E.

> The Pantheon is the largest building from ancient Rome that survives intact.

The Roman emperor Caligula made his horse a senator.

> The Roman emperor Commodos collected all the dwarfs, cripples, and freaks he could find and had them brought to the Colosseum, where they were ordered to fight each other to the death with meat cleavers.

The saying "It's all fun and games until someone loses an eye" is from ancient Rome. The only rule during wrestling matches was no eye gouging. Everything else was allowed, but the only way to be disqualified was to poke someone's eyes out.

All office-seekers in the Roman Empire were obliged to wear a certain white toga for a period of one year before the election.

THE CHINA CLUB

Slaves under the last emperors of China wore pigtails so they could be picked out quickly.

The Chinese ideogram for *trouble* depicts two women living under one roof.

The Chinese Nationalist Golf Association claims the game is of Chinese origin (*ch'ui wan*—the ball-hitting game) from the third or second century B.C.E. There were official ordinances prohibiting a ball game with clubs in Belgium and Holland from 1360.

The Chinese, in historic times, used marijuana only as a remedy for dysentery.

The Great Wall of China, which is more than 2,500 miles long, took more than 1,700 years to build. There is enough stone in the Great Wall to build an eight-foot wall encircling the globe at the equator.

The world's youngest parents were eight and nine and lived in China in 1910.

IN THEIR PRIME

William Pitt, elected in 1783, was England's youngest prime minister at the age of only twenty-four.

Winston Churchill was born in a ladies' room during a dance.

"GREAT" WARS

During World War I, almost fourteen million people died in battle.

During World War I, cigarettes were handed out to soldiers along with their rations.

Charles de Gaulle's final words were "It hurts."

At age ninety, Peter Mustafic of Botovo, Yugoslavia, suddenly began speaking again after a silence of forty years. The Yugoslavian news agency quoted him as saying, "I just didn't want to do military service, so I stopped speaking in 1920; then I got used to it."

Prior to World War II, when guards were posted at the fence, anyone could wander right up to the front door of the White House.

A family of six died in Oregon during World War II as a result of a Japanese balloon bomb.

Corcoran jump boots (Army jump boots) have 82 stitches on the inside of the sole and 101 stitches on the outside of the sole in honor of the 82nd and 101st Airborne Divisions' actions during World War II.

During conscription for World War II, there were nine documented cases of men with three testicles.

It took the United States only four days to build a ship during World War II.

During World War II, the Navajo language was used successfully as a code by the United States.

W. C. Fields kept $50,000 in Germany "in case the little bastard wins."

World champion chess player Reuben Fine helped the United States calculate where enemy submarines might surface based on positional probability.

During World War II, Americans tried to train bats to drop bombs.

> Escape maps, compasses, and files were inserted into Monopoly game boards and smuggled into POW camps inside Germany during World War II; real money for escapees was slipped into the packs of Monopoly money.

"John has a long mustache" was the coded signal used by the French Resistance in World War II to mobilize their forces after the Allies had landed on the Normandy beaches.

> Kotex was first manufactured as bandages during World War II.

Playing cards were issued to British pilots in World War II. If captured, the cards could be soaked in water and unfolded to reveal a map for escape.

> The phrase "the whole nine yards" came from World War II fighter pilots in the Pacific. When arming their planes on the ground, the .50-caliber machine gun ammo belts measured exactly twenty-seven feet before being loaded into the fuselage. If the pilots fired all their ammo at a target, it got the whole nine yards.

The universally popular Hershey bar was used overseas during World War II as currency.

The very first bomb dropped by the Allies on Berlin during World War II killed the only elephant in the Berlin Zoo.

The Red Baron's real name was Manfred Von Richtofen.

The first atomic bomb dropped on Japan fell from the *Enola Gay*, named after the unit commander's mother. The second was dropped from a plane known as *Bock's Car*.

A B-25 bomber airplane crashed into the seventy-ninth floor of the Empire State Building on July 28, 1945.

HE SHOULD HAVE USED THE PATCH

The earliest recorded case of a man giving up smoking was on April 5, 1679, when Johan Katsu, sheriff of Turku, Finland, wrote in his diary, "I quit smoking tobacco." He died one month later.

SHIP OF DREAMS

Each anchor chain link on the *Titanic* was about 175 pounds.

The *Titanic* had four engines.

The *Titanic*'s radio call sign was "MGY."

The *Titanic* was running at twenty-two knots when she hit the iceberg.

Two dogs were among the *Titanic* survivors.

When the *Titanic* sunk, there were seventy-five hundred pounds of ham on it.

IT'S ALL ABOUT THE BENJAMINS

In 1968, a convention of beggars in Dacca, India, passed a resolution demanding that the minimum amount of alms be fixed at fifteen paisa (three cents).

AMERICAN HISTORY 101

More than 150 people were tried as witches and wizards in Salem, Massachusetts, in the late 1600s.

The $8 bill was designed and printed by Benjamin Franklin for the American Colonies.

During the American Revolution, many brides used to wear the color red instead of white as a symbol of rebellion.

Morocco was the first country to recognize the United States in 1789.

John Hancock was the only one of fifty signatories of the Declaration of Independence who actually signed it in July.

The first aerial photograph was taken from a balloon during the Civil War.

The Civil War was the first war in which news from the front was published within hours of its occurrence.

When John Wilkes Booth leaped on to the stage after shooting President Lincoln, he tripped on the American flag.

Robert E. Lee, of the Confederate Army, remains the only person, to date, to have graduated from the West Point military academy without a single demerit.

Robert E. Lee wore size 4½ shoe.

All the officers in the Confederate Army were given copies of *Les Misérables* by Victor Hugo to carry with them at all times. Robert E. Lee, among others, believed the book symbolized their cause. Both revolts were defeated.

Banks first used Scotch tape to mend torn currency during the Depression.

If a family had two or fewer servants in the United States in 1900, census takers recorded the family as lower middle class.

In 1954, boxers and wrestlers had to swear under oath they were not Communists before they could compete in the state of Indiana.

When Saigon fell, the signal for all Americans to evacuate was Bing Crosby's "White Christmas" being played on the radio.

THROUGH THE YEARS

In 1801, 20 percent of the people in the United States were slaves.

In 1829, two sisters in the United States, Susan and Deborah, weighed 205 and 124 pounds although they were only five and three years old, respectively.

In 1900, the third leading cause of death was diarrhea.

In 1917, Margaret Sanger was jailed for one month for establishing the first birth control clinic.

In 1937, yeast sales reached $20 million a year in the United States.

IT'S THE FASHION

Before the 1800s, there were no separately designed shoes for right and left feet.

Any Russian man who wore a beard was required to pay a special tax during the time of Peter the Great.

Children in the Chinook Indian tribe were strapped between boards from head to toe so they would have fashionably flat skulls.

Evidence of shoemaking exists as early as 10000 B.C.E.

In 1778, fashionable women of Paris never went out in blustery weather without a lightning rod attached to their hats.

In the marriage ceremony of the ancient Inca Indians of Peru, the couple was considered officially wed when they took off their sandals and handed them to each other.

Olive oil was used for washing the body in the ancient Mediterranean world.

Pirates thought having an earring would improve their eyesight.

Welsh mercenary bowmen in the medieval period only wore one shoe at a time.

Until the Middle Ages, underwater divers near the Mediterranean coastline collected golden strands from the pen shell, which used the strands to hold itself in place. The strands were woven into a luxury textile and made into ladies' gloves so fine that a pair could be packed into an empty walnut shell.

In Ethiopia, both males and females of the Surma tribes shave their heads as a mark of beauty.

A BAD DAY TO GET OUT OF BED

The Korean War began on June 25, 1950.

The sinking of the German vessel *Wilhelm Gustloff* is the greatest sea disaster of all time. Approximately eight thousand people drowned.

In the Great Fire of London in 1666, half of London was burned down but only six people were injured.

Influenza caused more than twenty million deaths in 1918.

More than half a million people died as a result of the Spanish influenza epidemic.

 TGIF?

> In the nineteenth century, the British Navy attempted to dispel the superstition that Friday was an unlucky day to embark on a ship. The keel of a new ship was laid on a Friday; she was named HMS *Friday*, commanded by a Captain Friday, and finally went to sea on a Friday. Neither the ship nor her crew was ever heard of again.

GIVE PEACE A CHANCE

It has been calculated that in the last 3,500 years, there have been only 230 years of peace throughout the civilized world.

Spain declared war on the United States in 1898.

The Hundred Years' War lasted 116 years.

The shortest war in history was between Zanzibar and England in 1896. Zanzibar surrendered after thirty-eight minutes.

The Spanish Inquisition once condemned the entire Netherlands to death for heresy.

Those condemned to death by the axe in medieval and Renaissance England were obliged to tip their executioner to ensure that he would complete the job in one blow. In some executions, notably that of Mary, Queen of Scots, it took fifteen whacks of the blade before the head was severed.

To strengthen the Damascus sword, the blade was plunged into a slave.

Oliver Cromwell was hanged and decapitated two years after his death.

Close to seven hundred thousand land mines were dug up from the banks of the Suez Canal after the 1973 war between Egypt and Israel.

🌰 NOBLE NOBEL

The Nobel Prize was first awarded in 1901. It resulted from a late change in the will of Alfred Nobel, who did not want to be remembered after his death as a propagator of violence—he invented dynamite.

RUSSIAN ROULETTE

Czar Paul I banished soldiers to Siberia for marching out of step.

Russian I. M. Chisov survived a 21,980-foot plunge out of a plane with no parachute. He landed on the steep side of a snow-covered mountain.

STUCK IN THE MIDDLE (AGES) WITH YOU

During the Middle Ages, few people were able to read or write. The clergy were virtually the only ones who could.

During the Middle Ages, it was widely believed that men had one less rib than women. This is because of the story in the Bible that Eve had been created out of Adam's rib.

Everyone believed in the Middle Ages—as Aristotle had—that the heart was the seat of intelligence.

FIRST IN LINE

The actors in the first English play to be performed in America were arrested, as acting was considered evil.

Euripides was the first person on record to denounce slavery.

Income tax was first introduced in England in 1799 by British prime minister William Pitt.

Leif Erikson was the first European to set foot in North America, in 1000 C.E., *not* Columbus.

New Zealand was the first country to give women the vote, in 1890.

The first American in space was Alan B. Shepard Jr.

The Wright Brothers' first plane was called *The Bird of Prey*.

Orville Wright was involved in the first aircraft accident. His passenger, a Frenchman, was killed.

The first man ever to set foot on Antarctica was John Davis on February 7, 1821.

The first people to arrive on Iceland were Irish explorers in 795 C.E.

The first police force was established in Paris in 1667.

The first telephone book ever issued contained only fifty names. It was published in New Haven, Connecticut, by the New Haven District Telephone Company, in February 1878.

SKEWED BELIEFS

In Puritan times, to be born on a Sunday was interpreted as a sign of great sin.

In the 1700s in London, you could purchase insurance against going to hell.

In Victorian times, there was an intense fear of being buried alive. So when someone died, a small hole was dug from the casket to the surface, then a string was tied around the dead person's finger, which was then attached to a small but loud bell hung on the surface of the grave. If someone was buried alive, they could ring the bell and whoever was on duty would go and dig them up. Someone was on the duty twenty-four hours a day—hence the graveyard shift.

Long ago, the people of Nicaragua believed that if they threw beautiful young women into a volcano it would stop erupting.

In 1982, the last member of a group of people who believed the earth was hollow died.

WRONGFUL DEATH

Hrand Araklein, a Brink's car guard, was killed when $50,000 worth of quarters fell on and crushed him.

In 1911, Bobby Beach broke nearly all the bones in his body after surviving a barrel ride over Niagara Falls. Some time later in New Zealand, he slipped on a banana and died from the fall.

A fierce gust of wind blew forty-five-year-old Vittorio Luise's car into a river near Naples, Italy, in 1980. He managed to break a window, climb out, and swim to shore, where a tree blew over and killed him.

THE NEW WORLD

It costs more to buy a car today than it cost Christopher Columbus to equip and undertake three voyages to the New World.

It is estimated that within twenty years of Columbus discovering the New World, the Spaniards killed off 1.5 million Native Americans.

Native Americans never actually ate turkey; killing such a timid bird was thought to indicate laziness.

Pilgrims ate popcorn at the first Thanksgiving dinner.

NATIONAL SING-A-LONGS

The national anthem of Greece has 158 verses.

The national anthem of the Netherlands, "Het Wilhel-
mus," is an acrostichon. The first letters of each of the
fifteen verses represent the name Willem Van Nassov.

Francis Scott Key was a young lawyer who wrote the
poem "The Star Spangled Banner" after being inspired by
watching the Americans fight off the British attack of Baltimore during the War of 1812. The poem became the
words to the national anthem.

The Netherlands and the United States both have an-
thems that do not mention their countries' names.

The Japanese national anthem has the oldest lyrics/text,
from the ninth century, but the music is from 1880.

ADDICTED TO YOU

In 1865, opium was grown in the state of Virginia and a
product was distilled from it that yielded 4 percent mor-
phine. In 1867, it was grown in Tennessee; six years later it

was cultivated in Kentucky. During these years, opium, marijuana, and cocaine could be purchased legally over the counter from any chemist.

> One of the reasons marijuana is illegal today is because cotton growers in the 1930s lobbied against hemp farmers—they saw hemp as competition. It is not chemically addictive, as is nicotine, alcohol, or caffeine.

Nicotine was introduced by Jean Nicot (French ambassador to Portugal) in France in 1560.

ROAM IF YOU WANT TO

ON THE ROAD AGAIN . . .

One hundred sixty cars can drive side by side on the Monumental Axis in Brazil, the world's widest road.

The highest motorway in England is the M62 Liverpool to Hull. At its peak, it reaches 1,221 feet above sea level over the Saddleworth Moor, the burial ground of the victims of the infamous Myra Hindley, Moors Murderer.

Built in 1697, the Frankford Avenue Bridge, which crosses Pennypack Creek in Philadelphia, is the oldest U.S. bridge in continuous use.

The Golden Gate Bridge was first opened in 1937.

According to the Texas Department of Transportation, one person is killed annually painting stripes on the state's highways and roads.

IF YOU BUILD IT, THEY WILL COME

Construction on the Leaning Tower of Pisa began on August 9, 1173. There are 296 steps to the top.

> The Hoover Dam was built to last two thousand years. The concrete in it will not even be fully cured for another five hundred years.

In Washington, D.C., no building can be built taller than the Washington Monument.

> The Pentagon in Arlington, Virginia, has five sides, five stories, and five acres in the middle.

At one point, the Circus Maximus in Rome could hold up to 250,000 people.

> Buckingham Palace has more than six hundred rooms.

The foundations of many great European cathedrals are as deep as forty to fifty feet.

At one point, the Panama Canal was going to be built in Nicaragua.

In Calcutta, 79 percent of the population lives in one-room houses.

 **EI-FFEL AWFUL**

The Eiffel Tower was built for the 1889 World's Fair. The blueprints covered more than fourteen thousand square feet of drafting paper. The Eiffel Tower has 2.5 million rivets, and its height varies as much as six inches, depending on the temperature.

NAME GAME

Los Angeles's full name is El Pueblo de Nuestra Senora la Reina de los Angeles de Porciuncula and can be abbreviated to 6.3 percent of its size: L.A.

There is a place in Norway called Hell.

There is a resort town in New Mexico called Truth or Consequences.

There is a town in Texas called Ding Dong.

There is an airport in Calcutta named Dum Dum Airport.

There was once a town named 6 in West Virginia.

There's a cemetery town in California called Colma; its ratio of dead to living people is 750 to 1.

If you come from Manchester, you are a Manchurian.

Nova Scotia is Latin for "New Scotland."

The abbreviation ORD for Chicago's O'Hare Airport comes from the old name Orchard Field.

. . . OR MAYBE NOT

The slogan on New Hampshire license plates is "Live Free or Die." These license plates are manufactured by prisoners in the state prison in Concord.

SOME STIFF FIGURES

If a statue of a person on a horse depicts the horse with both front legs in the air, the person died in battle; if the horse has one front leg in the air, the person died as a result of wounds received in battle; if the horse has all four legs on the ground, the person died of natural causes.

The Sphinx at Giza in Egypt is 240 feet long and carved out of limestone. Built by Pharaoh Khafre to guard the way to his pyramid, it has a lion's body and the ruler's head.

The name of the Statue of Liberty is Mother of Exiles. Printed on the book the statue is holding is "July IV, MDCCLXXVI." The statue's mouth is three feet wide.

The names of the two stone lions in front of the New York Public Library are Patience and Fortitude. They were named by the then-mayor Fiorello La-Guardia.

Worldwide, there are more statues of Joan of Arc than of anyone else. France alone has about forty thousand of them.

SCHOOL DAYS

The University of Alaska stretches across four time zones.

The main library at Indiana University sinks more than an inch every year because when it was built, engineers failed to take into account the weight of all the books that would occupy the building.

Harvard uses Yale brand locks on their buildings; Yale uses Best brand.

Harvard is the oldest university in the United States.

DO YOU HAVE THE TIME?

There are no clocks in Las Vegas gambling casinos.

The shopping mall in Abbotsford, British Columbia, has the largest water clock in North America.

The clock at the National Bureau of Standards in Washington, D.C., will gain or lose only one second in three hundred years because it uses cesium atoms.

ON DISPLAY

The Liberace Museum has a mirror-plated Rolls Royce; jewel-encrusted capes; and the largest rhinestone in the world, weighing fifty-nine pounds and measuring almost a foot in diameter.

The Future's Museum in Sweden contains a scale model of the solar system. The sun is 105 meters in diameter, and the planets range from 5 millimeters to

6 kilometers from the sun. This particular model also contains the nearest star Proxima Centauri, still to scale, situated in the Museum of Victoria . . . in Australia.

WORLD OF WONDERS

No white man saw the Grand Canyon until after the Civil War. It was first entered on May 29, 1869, by the geologist John Wesley Powell.

The Taj Mahal was actually built for use as a tomb. It was scheduled to be torn down in the 1830s.

It is forbidden to fly aircraft over the Taj Mahal.

Due to precipitation, for a few weeks each year K2 is taller than Mt. Everest.

If you divide the Great Pyramid's perimeter by two times its height, you get pi to the fifteenth digit.

The Great Wall stretches for 4,160 miles across North China.

The Angel Falls in Venezuela are nearly twenty times taller than Niagara Falls.

🌰 PERHAPS YOU WERE MISTAKEN

The many sights that represent the Chinese city of Beijing were built by foreigners: the Forbidden City was built by the Mongols, the Temple of Heaven by the Manchurians.

Three Mile Island is only 2.5 miles long.

I WANT TO BE A PART OF IT . . .

All the dirt from the foundation to build the World Trade Center in New York City was dumped into the Hudson River to form the community now known as Battery City Park.

The amusement park Coney Island has had three of its rides designated as New York City historical landmarks.

Central Park opened in 1876. It is nearly twice the size of the entire country of Monaco.

The 102-story Empire State Building, completed in 1931, is made up of more than 10 million bricks and has 6,500 windows. It was built at a cost of $40,948,900.

CALIFORNIA DREAMIN'

Since the 1930s, the town of Corona, California, has lost all seventeen of the time capsules they originally buried.

The San Diego Zoo has the largest collection of animals in the world.

The San Francisco cable cars are the only mobile national monuments.

The largest object ever found in the Los Angeles sewer system was a motorcycle.

LOCAL CUSTOMS

If you bring a raccoon's head to the Henniker, New Hampshire, town hall, you are entitled to receive ten dollars from the town.

In 1980, a Las Vegas hospital suspended workers for betting on when patients would die.

There's a bathroom in Egypt where it is free to use the toilet, but you have to bring or buy your own toilet paper.

Some hotels in Las Vegas have gambling tables float-ing in their swimming pools.

WELL, AT LEAST WE'RE NUMBER ONE IN SOMETHING . . .

As of April 2000, Hong Kong had 392,000 fax lines—one of the highest rates of business fax use in the world.

Maine is the toothpick capital of the world.

ADD IT UP

Forty-seven czars are buried within the Kremlin.

Fifty-seven countries were involved in World War II.

There are 3,900 islands in Japan, the country of islands.

HOLY MATTERS

DIFFERING OPINIONS

Christianity has more than a billion followers. Islam is next in representation, with half this number.

The Norsemen considered the mistletoe a baleful plant that caused the death of Baldur, the shining god of youth.

In Turkey, the color of mourning is violet. In most Muslim countries and in China, it is white.

Voodoo originated in Haiti.

MONK-EYING AROUND

Ukrainian monk Dionysius Exiguus created the modern-day Christian calendar.

The monastic hours are matins, lauds, prime, tierce, sext, nones, vespers, and compline.

HOLY MOLY

The practice of exchanging presents at Christmas originated with the Romans.

The three cardinal virtues are faith, hope, and charity.

It was only after 440 C.E. that December 25 was celebrated as the birth date of Jesus Christ.

Two-thirds of Portugal was owned by the Church in the early eighteenth century.

Kerimaki Church in Finland is the world's largest church made of wood.

Las Vegas has the most chapels per capita than any other U.S. city.

Sister Boom-Boom was a transvestite nun who ran for mayor of San Francisco in 1982. He/she received more than twenty thousand votes.

St. Stephen is the patron saint of bricklayers.

IS THE POPE CATHOLIC?

Pope Adrian VI died after a fly got stuck in his throat as he was drinking from a water fountain.

The youngest pope was eleven years old.

The election of a new pope is announced to the world with white smoke.

Pope Paul IV, who was elected on May 23, 1555, was so outraged when he saw the naked bodies on the ceiling of the Sistine Chapel that he ordered Michelangelo to paint clothes on them.

OY VEY!

According to ceremonial customs of Orthodox Judaism, it is officially sundown when you cannot tell the difference between a black thread and a red thread.

A young shepherd boy discovered the Dead Sea Scrolls at Qumran, Jordan, in 1947.

Snow angels originated from medieval Jewish mystics who practiced rolling in the snow to purge themselves of evil urges.

BUDDHA-OLOGY

Contrary to popular belief, there are almost no Buddhists in India, nor have there been for about a thousand years. Although Buddhism was founded in India around 470 B.C.E. and developed there at an early date, it was uprooted from India between the seventh and twelfth centuries C.E. and today exists almost exclusively outside the country, primarily in Sri Lanka, Japan, and Indochina.

A temple in Sri Lanka is dedicated to one of the Buddha's teeth.

HINDU WHO?

Hindu men once believed it to be unlucky to marry a third time. They could avoid misfortune by marrying a tree first. The tree (the third wife) was then burned, freeing the man to marry again.

Husbands and wives in India who desire children whisper their wish in the ear of a sacred cow.

On the stone temples of Madura in southern India, there are more than thirty million carved images of gods and goddesses.

IT'S A PARTY

A third of Taiwanese funeral processions include a stripper.

BUSINESS RELATIONS

BRANDING THE COW

A single share of Coca-Cola stock purchased in 1919, when the company went public, would have been worth $92,500 in 1997.

IBM's motto is "Think."

NERF, the popular foam children's toy company, doesn't actually stand for anything.

Nestlé is the largest company in Switzerland, yet more than 98 percent of its revenue comes from outside the country.

The three most valuable brand names on Earth are Marlboro, Coca-Cola, and Budweiser, in that order.

THEY'RE IN THE MONEY

Japan's currency is the most difficult to counterfeit.

John D. Rockefeller was the first billionaire in the United States.

Howard Hughes once made half a billion dollars in one day. In 1966, he received a bank draft for $546,549,171 in return for his 75 percent holdings in TWA.

Ted Turner owns 5 percent of New Mexico.

Organized crime is estimated to account for 10 percent of the United States' national income.

LOSE SOME TO MAKE SOME

It takes about sixty-three thousand trees to make the newsprint for the average Sunday edition of *The New York Times*.

The average bank cashier loses $310 a year.

THE JOB MARKET

Sixty percent of big-firm executives say the cover letter is as important as or more important than the résumé itself when you're looking for a new job.

The largest employer in the world is the Indian railway system, employing more than a million people.

The most dangerous job in the United States is that of sanitation worker. Fire fighters and police officers are a close second and third, followed by leather tanners in fourth.

COMPANY POLICY

Workers at Matsushita Electric Company in Japan beat dummies of their foremen with bamboo sticks to let off steam. The company has enjoyed 30 percent growth for 25 consecutive years.

SELLER'S MARKET

The sale of vodka makes up 10 percent of Russian government income.

In most advertisements, including newspapers, the time displayed on a watch is 10:10.

THE SPORTING GOODS

YOU'RE OUT!

Fifty-six million people go to Major League baseball games each year.

A baseball has exactly 108 stitches.

Babe Ruth wore a cabbage leaf under his hat to keep his head cool. He changed it every two innings.

Bank robber John Dillinger played professional baseball.

Baseball games between college teams have been played since the Civil War.

Baseball was the first sport to be pictured on the cover of *Sports Illustrated* magazine.

Baseball's home plate is seventeen inches wide.

Before 1859, baseball umpires used to sit in rocking chairs behind home plate.

It takes about eight seconds to make a baseball bat in a baseball bat factory.

The first formal rules for playing baseball required the winning team to score twenty-one runs.

NOTHING BUT NET

Basketball was invented by Canadian James Naismith in 1891.

The theme song of the Harlem Globetrotters is "Sweet Georgia Brown."

I WANT TO BE LIKE . . .

Michael Jordan makes more money from Nike annually than all the Nike factory workers in Malaysia combined.

Michael Jordan shaves his head on Tuesdays and Fridays.

RUN ON

In 1936, American track star Jesse Owens beat a racehorse over a one-hundred-yard course. The horse was given a head start.

Sprinters on track teams started taking a crouching start in 1908.

The expression "getting someone's goat" is based on the custom of keeping a goat in the stable with a racehorse as the horse's companion. The goat becomes a settling influence for the Thoroughbred. If you owned a competing horse and were not above some dirty business, you could steal your rival's goat (it's been done) to upset the other horse and make it run a poor race.

Anise is the scent on the artificial rabbit that is used in greyhound races.

BEND IT LIKE BECKHAM

Bulgaria was the only soccer team in the 1994 World Cup in which all the players' last names ended with the letters "ov."

Soccer is played in more countries than any other sport.

Soccer legend Pele's real name is Edson Arantes do Nascimento.

The band Simply Red is named for its love for the soccer team Manchester United, which has a red home strip.

BLUE 42! HUT!

Green Bay Packers backup quarterback Matt Hasselbeck has been struck by lightning twice in his life.

It takes three thousand cows to supply the NFL with enough leather for a year's supply of footballs.

An American football has four seams.

O. J. Simpson had a severe case of rickets and wore leg braces when he was a child.

The Super Bowl is broadcast in 182 countries. That is more than 88 percent of the countries in the world.

When the University of Nebraska Cornhuskers play football at home, the stadium becomes the state's third largest city.

FORE!

Rudyard Kipling, living in Vermont in the 1890s, invented the game of snow golf. He painted his golf balls red so he could locate them in the snow.

Americans spend more than $630 million a year on golf balls.

Before 1850, golf balls were made of leather and stuffed with feathers.

The fastest round of golf (18 holes) by a team was 9 minutes, 28 seconds, a record set in Worcester on September 9, 1996, at 10:40 A.M.

Golfing great Ben Hogan's famous reply when asked how to improve one's game was, "Hit the ball closer to the hole."

In the United States, there are more than ten thousand golf courses.

Many Japanese golfers carry hole-in-one insurance, because it is traditional in Japan to share one's good luck by sending gifts to all your friends when you get an ace. The price for what the Japanese term "an albatross" can often reach $10,000.

Pro golfer Wayne Levi was the first PGA pro to win a tournament using a colored (orange) ball. He did it in the Hawaiian Open.

Twelve new golf holes are constructed every day.

The only person ever to play golf on the moon was Alan Shepard. His golf ball was never found.

The Tom Thumb golf course was the first miniature golf course in the United States. It was built it 1929 in Chattanooga, Tennessee, by John Garnet Carter.

The United States Golf Association was founded in 1894 as the governing body of golf in the United States.

The youngest golfer recorded to have shot a hole-in-one is five-year-old Coby Orr of Littleton, Colorado, on the 103-yard fifth hole at the Riverside Golf Course in San Antonio, Texas, in 1975.

A regulation golf ball has 336 dimples.

Two golf clubs claim to be the first established in the United States: the Foxberg Golf Club in Clarion County, Pennsylvania (1887), and St. Andrews Golf Club of Yonkers, New York (1888).

KNOCK OUT

Boxing is considered the easiest sport for gamblers to fix.

Boxing rings are so called because they used to be round.

In 1985, Mike Tyson started boxing professionally at age eighteen.

Boxing is the most popular sport to create a film about.

Four men in the history of boxing have been knocked out in the first eleven seconds of the first round.

OLYMPIC FANFARE

Canada is the only country not to win a gold medal in the Summer Olympic Games while hosting the event.

Only two countries have participated in every modern Olympic Games: Greece and Australia.

The 1900 Olympics were held in Paris, France.

Tug-of-war was an Olympic event between 1900 and 1920.

The five Olympic rings represent the continents.

Olympic badminton rules say that the birdie has to have exactly fourteen feathers.

The city of Denver was chosen to host and then refused the 1976 Winter Olympics.

FISHING FOR SWIMMERS

A top freestyle swimmer achieves a speed of only four miles per hour. Fish, in contrast, have been clocked at sixty-eight miles per hour.

Captain Matthew Webb of England was the first to swim the English Channel using the breaststroke.

SURPRISING SPORTS

In the United States, more Frisbee discs are sold each year than baseballs, basketballs, and footballs combined.

Kite-flying is a professional sport in Thailand.

There are at least two sports in which the team has to move backward to win—tug-of-war and rowing.

Badminton used to be called "Poona."

PIN AND CONQUER

The national sport of Japan is sumo wrestling.

Morihei Ueshiba, founder of Aikido, once pinned a sumo wrestler using only a single finger.

Nearly all sumo wrestlers have flat feet and big bottoms.

The 1912 Greco-Roman wrestling match in Stockholm between Finn Alfred Asikainen and Russian Martin Klein lasted more than eleven hours.

LORDS OF THE ICE

A hockey puck is one inch thick.

Canada imports about 850 Russian-made hockey sticks on an average day.

Professional hockey players skate at average speeds of twenty to twenty-five miles per hour.

ON STRIKES

Three consecutive strikes in bowling are called a turkey.

Tokyo has the world's largest bowling alley.

The bowling ball was invented in 1862.

FIRST CONTACT

The game of squash originated in the United Kingdom.

Australian Rules Football was originally designed to give cricketers something to play during the off-season.

Karate actually originated in India.

DANGEROUS GAMES

The only bone not broken so far during any ski accident is one located in the inner ear.

AND THE HEAVYWEIGHT CHAMPION OF THE WORLD IS . . .

Sports Illustrated has the largest sports magazine circulation.

AND MAYBE THIS IS WHY . . .

Cathy Rigby is the only woman to pose nude for *Sports Illustrated*.

THROW THE GAME

A forfeited game in baseball is recorded as a 9–0 score. In football, it is recorded as a 1–0 score.

TEAM SPIRIT

In the four professional major North American sports (baseball, basketball, football, and hockey), only eight teams' nicknames do not end with "s." These teams are the Miami Heat, the Utah Jazz, the Orlando Magic, the Boston Red Sox, the Chicago White Sox, the Colorado Avalanche, the Tampa Bay Lightning, and the Minnesota Wild.

I'M SO HIGH RIGHT NOW . . .

Pole vault poles used to be stiff. Now they bend, which allows the vaulter to go much higher.

SCIENTIFICALLY SPEAKING

AMAZING DISCOVERIES

A device invented as a primitive steam engine by the Greek engineer Hero, about the time of the birth of Christ, is used today as a rotating lawn sprinkler.

Construction workers' hard hats were first invented and used in the building of the Hoover Dam in 1933.

Leonardo da Vinci invented the concept of the parachute, but his design was fatally flawed in that it did not allow air to pass through the top of the chute. Therefore, the chute would not fall straight, but would tilt to the side, lose its air, and plummet. He also invented the scissors.

Thomas Edison, the inventor of the lightbulb, was afraid of the dark.

NOT-SO-GREAT MOMENTS

The first atomic bomb exploded at Trinity Site, New Mexico.

India tested its first nuclear bomb in 1974.

A WEATHER EYE

A normal raindrop falls at about seven miles per hour.

A downburst is a downward-blowing wind that sometimes comes blasting out of a thunderstorm. The damage looks like tornado damage, because the wind can be as strong as an F2 tornado, but debris is blown straight away from a point on the ground, not lifted into the air and transported downwind.

A wind with a speed of seventy-four miles per hour or more is designated a hurricane.

An inch of snow falling evenly on 1 acre of ground is equivalent to about 2,715 gallons of water.

At any given time, there are eighteen hundred thunderstorms in progress over the earth's atmosphere.

A cubic mile of fog is made up of less than a gallon of water.

The two hottest months at the equator are March and September.

A rainbow can only occur when the sun is forty degrees or less above the horizon.

Meteorologists claim they're right 85 percent of the time.

ROCKETMEN

Astronauts in orbit around the earth can see the wakes of ships.

Buzz Aldrin's mother's maiden name was Moon.

Buzz Aldrin was the first man to pee his pants on the moon.

Neil Armstrong stepped on the moon with his left foot first.

The first man to return safely from space was Yuri Gagarin.

Three astronauts manned each *Apollo* flight.

The *Saturn V* moon rocket consumed fifteen tons of fuel per second.

The *Apollo 11* had only twenty seconds of fuel left when it landed.

The external tank on the space shuttle is not painted.

A manned rocket can reach the moon in less time than it took a stagecoach to travel the length of England.

Valentina Tereshkova was the first woman to enter space.

A SPACE ODYSSEY

All the stars in the Milky Way revolve around the center of the galaxy every two hundred million years.

Astronomers classify stars by their spectra.

Three stars make up Orion's belt.

French astronomer Adrien Auzout once considered building a telescope that was one thousand feet long in the 1600s. He thought the magnification would be so great he would see animals on the moon.

A neutron star has such a powerful gravitational pull that it can spin on its axis in one-thirtieth of a second without tearing itself apart. A pulsar is a neutron star, and it gets its energy from its rotation.

Stars come in different colors; hot stars give off blue light, and the cooler stars give off red light.

Earth is traveling through space at 660,000 miles per hour.

🌰 MOON RIVER

A full moon always rises at sunset.

A full moon is nine times brighter than a half moon.

February 1865 is the only month in recorded history not to have a full moon.

Carolyn Shoemaker has discovered thirty-two comets and approximately three hundred asteroids.

Any free-moving liquid in outer space will form itself into a sphere because of its surface tension.

The total quantity of energy in the universe is constant.

If you attempted to count the stars in a galaxy at a rate of one every second, it would take around three thousand years to count them all.

A syzygy occurs when three astronomical bodies line up.

The sixteenth-century astronomer Tycho Brahe lost his nose in a duel with one of his students over a mathematical computation. He wore a silver replacement nose for the rest of his life.

🌰 HERE COMES THE SUN

By weight, the sun is 70 percent hydrogen; 28 percent helium; 1.5 percent carbon, nitrogen, and oxygen; and 0.5 percent all other elements.

It takes eight and a half minutes for light to get from the sun to Earth. All totaled, the sunlight that strikes Earth at any given moment weighs as much as an ocean liner.

Galileo became totally blind just before his death. This is probably because of his constant gazing at the sun through his telescope.

Sunbeams that shine down through clouds are called crepuscular rays.

THE ELECTRIC SLIDE

One of the first lightbulbs was a thread of sheep's wool coated with carbon.

A bolt of lightning can strike the earth with a force as great as one hundred million volts and generates temperatures five times hotter than those found on the sun's surface.

You are more likely to lose your hearing than any of the other senses if you are hit by lightning.

TECHNOLOGICALLY ADVANCED

The first computer ever made was called ENIAC. A silicon chip a quarter-inch square has the capacity of the original 1949 ENIAC computer, which occupied a city block.

In 1961, MIT student Steve Russell created Spacewars, the first interactive computer game, on a Digital PDP-1 (Programmed Data Processor-1) mainframe computer. Limited by the computer technology of the time, ASCII text characters were the "graphics" and people could only play the game on a device that took up the floor space of a small house.

In 1949, forecasting the relentless march of science, *Popular Mechanics* said computers in the future may weigh no more than five tons.

Approximately 98 percent of software in China is pirated.

Back in the mid to late 1980s, an IBM-compatible computer wasn't considered 100 percent compatible unless it could run Microsoft's Flight Simulator.

Toronto was the first city in the world with a computerized traffic signal system.

The first product Motorola started to develop was a record player for automobiles. At that time, the most well-known player on the market was the Victrola, so they called themselves Motorola.

Experts at Intel say that microprocessor speed will double every eighteen months for at least ten years.

A third of ninety-five developing countries have a waiting period of six years or more for a telephone connection, compared with less than a month in developed countries.

When CBS broadcast the first television show in color, no one other than CBS owned a color television set.

In 1977, Cairo only had 208,000 telephones and no telephone books.

THE THIRD "R"

All snow crystals are hexagonal.

An enneahedron is solid with nine faces.

The billionth digit of pi is nine.

René Descartes came up with the theory of coordinate geometry by looking at a fly walk across a tiled ceiling.

LEAVING ON A JET PLANE

A jumbo jet uses four thousand gallons of fuel to take off.

A Boeing 747's wingspan is longer than the distance of the Wright Brothers' first flight.

The tail section of an airplane gives the bumpiest ride.

The condensed water vapor left by jets in the sky is called a contrail.

American Airlines saved $40,000 in 1987 by eliminating one olive from each salad served in first class.

The Boeing 737 jet is nicknamed "Fat Albert."

The Boeing 747 has been in commercial service since 1970.

The shortest intercontinental commercial flight in the world is from Gibraltar in Europe to Tangier in Africa at a distance of thirty-four miles and a flight time of twenty minutes.

I FEEL THE EARTH MOVE

April is Earthquake Preparedness Month. For a little added incentive, consider this: the most powerful earthquake to strike the United States occurred in 1811 in New Madrid, Missouri. The quake shook more than one million square miles and was felt as far as one thousand miles away.

A REAL GEM

A large, flawless emerald is worth more than a similarly large flawless diamond.

Gold was the first metal to be discovered. South Africa produces two-thirds of the world's gold. All the gold produced in the past five hundred years, if melted, could be compressed into a fifty-foot cube. A lump of pure gold the size of a Matchbox car can be flattened into a sheet the size of a tennis court. India has the world's largest stock of privately hoarded gold.

Diamonds are composed of just one chemical element, carbon. The color of diamond dust is black. According to the Gemological Institute of America, up until 1896, India was the only source of diamonds in the world.

The company Kodak is the largest user of silver.

GREEN THUMB

Bamboo (the world's tallest grass) can grow up to ninety centimeters in a day.

It takes the insect-eating Venus flytrap plant only half a second to shut its trap on its prey. The Venus flytrap can eat a whole cheeseburger.

The Siberian larch accounts for more than 20 percent of all the world's trees.

The Sitka spruce is Britain's most commonly planted tree.

The Saguaro Cactus, found in the southwestern United States, doesn't grow branches until it is seventy-five years old.

The leaves of the Victorian water lily are sometimes more than six feet in diameter.

The bark of a redwood tree is fireproof. Fires that occur in a redwood forest take place inside the trees.

Orchids are grown from seeds so small it would take thirty thousand to weigh as much as one grain of wheat.

It takes one fifteen- to twenty-year-old tree to produce seven hundred paper grocery bags.

One ragweed plant can release as many as one billion grains of pollen.

LET'S GET PHYSIC-AL

A cesium atom in an atomic clock beats 9,192,631,770 times a second.

A temperature of 70 million degrees Celsius was generated at Princeton University in 1978. This was during a fusion experiment and is the highest man-made temperature ever.

During the time that the atomic bomb was being hatched by the United States at Alamogordo, New Mexico, applicants for routine jobs like janitors were disqualified if they could read. Illiteracy was a job requirement. The reason: the authorities did not want their rubbish or other papers read.

The radioactive substance Americanium-241 is used in many smoke detectors.

The average life of a nuclear plant is forty years.

CHEMICAL REACTIONS

German chemist Hennig Brand discovered phosphorus while he was examining urine.

A "creep" is a metallurgical term for when something that is normally very strong bends because of gravity. This happens to many metals at high temperatures, where they won't melt but they will creep.

All organic compounds contain carbon.

Almost all the helium that exists in the world today is from natural gas wells in the United States.

DuPont is the world's largest chemical company.

Hydrogen is the most common atom in the universe.

Mercury is the only metal that is liquid at room temperature.

Methane gas can often be seen bubbling up from the bottom of ponds. It is produced by the decomposition of dead plants and animals in the mud.

The ashes of the metal magnesium are heavier than magnesium itself.

There are five trillion trillion atoms in one pound of iron.

The densest substance on Earth is the metal osmium.

The metal part at the end of a pencil is 20 percent sulfur.

The 111th element is known as unnilenilenium.

The U.S. Bureau of Standards says that the electron is the fastest thing in the world.

The shockwave from a nitroglycerine explosion travels at seventeen thousand miles per hour.

Marie Curie, the Nobel Prize–winning scientist who discovered radium, died on July 4, 1934, of radiation poisoning.

CHILLY WATERS

H_2O expands as it freezes and contracts as it melts, displacing the exact same amount of fluid in either state. So if the northern ice cap did melt, it would cause absolutely no rise in the level of the ocean.

Hot water is heavier than cold.

An iceberg contains more heat than a match.

WEIRD SCIENCE

One hundred seven incorrect medical procedures will be performed by the end of the day today.

Because of the rotation of the earth, an object can be thrown farther if it is thrown west.

Two and five are the only prime numbers that end in two or five.

Fifty-one percent of turns are right turns.

If you toss a penny 10,000 times, it will not be heads 5,000 times but more like 4,950. The head picture weighs more, so it ends up on the bottom.

If you yelled for eight years, seven months, and six days, you would have produced enough sound energy to heat one cup of coffee.

The strength of early lasers was measured in Gillettes, the number of blue razor blades a given beam could puncture.

The tip of a bullwhip moves so fast that it breaks the sound barrier; the crack of the whip is actually a tiny sonic boom.

Clouds fly higher during the day than at night.

Moisture, not air, causes superglue to dry.

Recycling one glass jar saves enough energy to power a TV for three hours.

Iron nails cannot be used in oak because the acid in the wood corrodes them.

Bacteria, the tiniest free-living cells, are so small that a single drop of liquid contains as many as fifty million of them.

Life on Earth probably developed in an oxygen-free atmosphere. Even today there are microorganisms that can live only in the absence of oxygen.

Stainless steel was discovered by accident in 1913.

If we had the same mortality rate as in the 1900s, more than half the people in the world today would not be alive.

SYNTHETIC MATERIALS

Edmonton, Canada, was the first city in North America with a population of less than one million to open a Light Rail Transit System, in 1978.

Russia built more than ten thousand miles of railroad between 1896 and 1900.

The U.S. standard railroad gauge (the distance between rails) is 4 feet, 8.5 inches.

A fully loaded supertanker traveling at normal speed takes at least twenty minutes to stop.

The first American submarine was built around 1776.

About seven million cars are junked each year in the United States.

Robots in Japan pay union dues.

The metal instrument used in shoe stores to measure feet is called the Brannock device.

The CN Tower in Toronto is the tallest free-standing structure in the world.

A standard grave measures 7'8" by 3'2" by 6'.

Man releases more than a billion tons of pollutants into the earth's atmosphere every year.

EXPERT TIMING

The smallest unit of time is the yoctosecond.

Twenty years make up a vicennial period.

At room temperature, the average air molecule travels at the speed of a rifle bullet.

A jiffy is an actual unit of time: one-hundredth of a second. Thus the saying, "I will be there in a jiffy!"

WILD KINGDOM

OH, BABY!

A baby baleen whale depends on its mother's milk diet for at least six months.

A baby bat is called a pup.

A baby blue whale is twenty-five feet long at birth.

A baby caribou is so swift it can easily outrun its mother when it is only three days old.

A baby platypus remains blind after birth for eleven weeks.

A baby beaver stays with its parents for a period of two years.

A baby giraffe is about six feet tall at birth.

A baby gray whale drinks enough milk to fill more than two thousand bottles a day.

It takes forty-two days for an ostrich egg to hatch.

It may take longer than two days for a chick to break out of its shell.

It takes twenty-four hours for a tiny newborn swan to peck its way out of its shell.

To be called a mammal, the female must feed her young on milk she has produced.

Wandering albatross devote a full year to raising their babies.

Surprisingly, when leaving their nests for the first time, chicks are very rarely hurt after falling to the ground.

Armadillos have four babies at a time, and they are always the same sex.

Kangaroos usually give birth to one young annually. The young kangaroo, or joey, is born alive at a very immature stage, when it is only about two centimeters long and weighs less than a gram.

The female blue crab can lay up to one million eggs in a day.

The female meadow vole can start reproducing when she is only twenty-five days old and gives birth to sixteen litters per year.

The female king crab incubates as many as four hundred thousand young for eleven months in a brood pouch under her abdomen.

The female American oyster lays an average of five hundred million eggs per year. Usually, only one oyster out of the bunch reaches maturity.

The American opossum, a marsupial, bears its young just twelve to thirteen days after conception.

The Asiatic elephant takes 608 days to give birth, or just over twenty months.

The anaconda, one of the world's largest snakes, gives birth to its young instead of laying eggs.

The gestation period for giraffes is about fourteen to fifteen months.

The male seahorse, not the female, carries the embryo of the species. The female fills the male's brooch pouch with eggs, which remain in the swollen sac for a gestation period of eight to ten days.

The only two mammals to lay eggs are the platypus and the echidna. The mothers nurse their babies through pores in their skin.

The Hirudo leech lays its babies within a cocoon; the Amazon leech carries its babies on its stomach—sometimes as many as three hundred at a time.

Every single hamster in the United States today comes from a single litter captured in Syria in 1930.

In 1859, twenty-four rabbits were released in Australia. Within six years, the population grew to two million.

THE MATING DANCE

Human beings and the two-toed sloth are the only land animals that typically mate face to face.

Iguanas, koalas, and Komodo dragons all have two penises.

A barnacle has the largest penis of any other animal in relation to its size.

In the past sixty years, the groundhog has only pre-
dicted the weather correctly 28 percent of the time.
The rushing back and forth from burrows is believed
to indicate sexual activity, not shadow seeking.

During the mating season, male porcupines bristle their
quills at each other and chatter their teeth in rage before
attacking. All porcupines at this time become very vocal:
grunting, whining, chattering, even barking and mewing
at each other.

Male boars form harems.

More than two million southern fur seals—95 percent of
the world's population—crowd onto the shores of South
Georgia Island each summer. Half the world's population of southern elephant seals also comes to the island to
mate.

Parthenogenesis is the term used to describe the process
by which certain animals are able to reproduce themselves in successive female generations without inter-
vention of a male of the species. At least one species of
lizard is known to do so.

The male fox mates for life and, if the female dies, he remains single for the rest of his life. However, if the male
dies, the female hooks up with a new mate.

The male house wren builds several nests as part of his courtship ritual. After the nests are completed, his potential bride looks them all over and then selects one as her preferred choice for the laying of her eggs.

The female salamander inseminates herself. At mating time, the male deposits a conical mass of a jellylike substance containing the sperm. The female draws the jelly into herself, and in so doing, fertilizes her eggs.

A female ferret will die if it goes into heat and cannot find a mate.

The female anglerfish is six times larger than her mate. The male anchors himself to the top of her head and stays there for the rest of his life. They literally become one. Their digestive and circulatory systems are merged. Except for two very large generative organs and a few fins, nothing remains of the male.

Starbuck, a Canadian bull who sired two hundred thousand dairy cows and an equal number of bulls in his life, earned an estimated $25 million before he died in 1998. After his death, his frozen semen was still selling for $250 a dose.

CREEPY CRAWLIES

An estimated 80 percent of creatures on Earth have six legs.

The first medical use of leeches dates back to approximately twenty-five hundred years ago. The leech's saliva contains a property that acts as an anticoagulant for human blood.

The leech has thirty-two brains.

The leech will gorge itself up to five times its body weight and then just fall off its victim. The Amazon leech uses a different method of sucking blood. It inserts a long proboscis into the victim as opposed to biting.

The Hirudo leech has three jaws with one hundred teeth on each jaw—making three hundred teeth in all.

A dragonfly has a life span of four to seven weeks.

A species of Australian dragonfly has been clocked at thirty-six miles per hour.

A species of earthworm in Australia grows up to ten feet in length.

A square mile of fertile earth has thirty-two million earthworms in it.

The longest species of earthworm is the *Megascolides australis*, found in Australia in 1868. An average specimen measures four feet in length, two feet when contracted, and seven feet when naturally extended.

Some ribbon worms will eat themselves if they cannot find food.

The nematode *Caenorhabditis elegans* ages the equivalent of five human years for every day they live, usually expiring after fourteen days. However, when stressed, the worm goes into a state of suspended animation that can last for two months or more. The human equivalent would be to sleep for about two hundred years.

The longest species of centipede is the giant scolopender (*Scolopendra gigantea*), found in the rain forests of Central and South America. It has twenty-three segments (forty-six legs), and specimens have been measured up to ten and a half inches long and one inch in diameter.

Caterpillars have about four thousand muscles. Humans, by comparison, have only about six hundred.

The average garden-variety caterpillar has 248 muscles in its head.

The original name for butterfly was the flutterby.

Butterflies taste with their hind feet.

Certain species of male butterflies produce scents that serve in attracting females during courtship.

The male gypsy moth can smell the virgin female gypsy moth from eight miles away.

A large swarm of locusts can eat eighty thousand tons of corn in a day.

After eating, the housefly regurgitates its food and eats it again.

Certain fireflies emit a light so penetrating that it can pass through flesh and wood.

Research indicates that mosquitoes are attracted to people who have recently eaten bananas.

The giant cricket of Africa enjoys eating human hair.

Grasshoppers have white blood.

Any female bee in a beehive could have been the queen if she had been fed the necessary royal jelly. All female bees in a given hive are sisters.

Bees do not have ears. Bees have five eyes: three small eyes on the top of a bee's head and two larger ones in front.

Male bees will try to attract sex partners with orchid fragrance.

A cockroach's favorite food is the glue on the back of stamps.

Small cockroaches are more likely to die on their backs than large cockroaches.

There is an average of fifty thousand spiders per acre in green areas.

A strand from the web of the golden spider is as strong as a steel wire of the same size.

Spider silk is an extremely strong material, and its on-weight basis has been proven to be stronger than steel. Experts suggest that a pencil-thick strand of silk could stop a Boeing 747 in flight.

Tarantulas cannot spin webs.

Tarantulas do not use muscles to move their legs. They control the amount of blood pumped into them to extend and retract their legs.

Tarantulas that are seen wandering around in the wild do not make good pets. These are sexually mature males at the end of their life cycle—they will die within a few weeks or months.

LEAPFROGS

It was discovered on a space mission that a frog can throw up. The frog throws up its stomach first, so the stomach is dangling out of its mouth. Then the frog uses its forearms to dig out all the stomach contents and then swallows the stomach back down.

The poison arrow frog has enough poison to kill about twenty-two hundred people.

Japan is the largest exporter of frogs' legs.

Certain frogs can be frozen solid, then thawed, and continue living.

Frog-eating bats identify edible from poisonous frogs by listening to the mating calls of male frogs. Frogs counter by hiding and using short, difficult-to-locate calls.

Frogs drink and breathe through their skin.

Frogs must close their eyes to swallow.

Some bullfrogs pretend to be dead when captured but quickly hop away when let go.

Tree frogs can climb windowpanes.

Several poison-dart frog species are bred at the National Aquarium in Baltimore. There, researchers gauge the toxicity of poisonous species by taste. No danger is posed, because frogs caught in the wild gradually become less poisonous, and captive offspring are nontoxic. The change may be due to diet. The frog's natural menu—mostly tropical ants and springtails—cannot be duplicated in a terrarium.

If a frog's mouth is held open for too long, the frog will suffocate.

The eyes and nose of a frog are on top of its head, enabling it to breathe and see when most of its body is under water.

Frogs move faster than toads.

Toads don't have teeth, but frogs do.

Golden toads are so rare that a biological reserve has been specifically created for them.

It is estimated that a single toad may catch and eat as many as ten thousand insects in the course of a summer.

Toads eat only moving prey.

LEAPIN' LIZARDS!

Reptiles are never slimy. Their scales have few glands and are usually silky to the touch.

Marine iguanas, saltwater crocodiles, sea snakes, and sea turtles are the only surviving seawater-adapted reptiles.

An iguana can stay under water for twenty-eight minutes.

Male western fence lizards do push-ups on tree limbs as a courtship display for females.

The Nile and Indo-Pacific saltwater crocodiles are the only two crocodiles that are considered true man-eaters.

The tuatara lizard of New Zealand has three eyes— two in the center of its head and one on top.

The tuatara's metabolism is so slow they only have to breathe once an hour.

The horned lizard of the American southwest may squirt a thin stream of blood from the corner of its eye when frightened.

The gecko lizard can run on the ceiling without falling because its toes have flaps of skin that act like suction cups.

Basilisks are frequently called Jesus Christ Lizards because of their ability to run on water.

The Ozark blind salamander begins life with eyes and plumelike gills. As the animal matures, its eyelids fuse together and the gills disappear.

A blind chameleon still changes color to match its environment.

A chameleon's tongue is twice the length of its body.

Each eye of the chameleon is independent of the other. The lizard can watch and study two totally different pictures at the same time.

The longest lizard in the world is the Komodo dragon at 10 feet long. The next longest are the water monitor at 8.8

feet, the perenty at 7.8 feet, the common iguana at 5 feet, and the marine iguana at 5 feet.

Komodo dragons eat deer and wild boar.

The first Komodo dragons to breed in the western world are at the National Zoo at the Smithsonian Institute in Washington, D.C.

The Gila monster spends about 96 percent of its life underground.

The girth of the Gila monster's tail may shrink by 80 percent during times of low food supply.

A crocodile's tongue is attached to the roof of its mouth.

More people are killed in Africa by crocodiles than by lions.

Estuarine crocodiles are the biggest of all twenty-six species of the crocodilian family.

To escape the grip of a crocodile's jaws, push your thumbs into its eyeballs. It will let you go instantly.

A newly hatched crocodile is three times as large as the egg from which it has emerged.

The Nile crocodile averages about forty-five years in the wild and may live up to eighty years in captivity.

Alligators cannot move backward.

In Michigan, it is illegal to chain an alligator to a fire hydrant.

Lorne Green had one of his nipples bitten off by an alligator while hosting an episode of *Lorne Green's Wild Kingdom*.

The word *alligator* comes from *El Lagarto*, which is Spanish for "The Lizard."

Unlike other reptiles, female alligators protect their young for up to two years after hatching.

SLITHERY SITUATIONS

The only continent without reptiles or snakes is Antarctica.

The gastric juices of a snake can digest bones and teeth—but not fur or hair.

Snakes do not urinate. They secrete and excrete uric acid, which is a solid, chalky, usually white substance.

Snakes, like cows, cannot activate their vitamin D without the presence of sunlight.

Snakes do not have eyelids, so even when they're asleep, they cannot close their eyes. They do have a protective layer of clear scales, called brille, over their eyes.

It takes about fifty hours for a snake to digest one frog.

Sidewinders are snakes that move by looping their bodies up in the air and pushing against the ground when they land. Their tracks in the ground would look like a series of straight lines angling in the direction the snake was traveling.

Rattlesnakes gather in groups to sleep through the winter. Sometimes up to one thousand of them coil up together to keep warm.

The poisonous copperhead smells like fresh-cut cucumbers.

Milk snakes lay about thirteen eggs—in piles of animal manure.

There are some fifty different species of sea snakes, and all of them are venomous. They thrive in abundance along the coast from the Persian Gulf to Japan and around Australia and Melanesia. Their venom is ten times as virulent as that of the cobra. Humans bitten by them have died within two-and-a-half hours.

The most venomous of all snakes, the Inland Taipan, has enough venom in one bite to kill more than two hundred thousand mice.

It takes approximately sixty-nine thousand venom extractions from the coral snake to fill a one-pint container.

Southern Indian drug addicts get high by having venomous snakes bite their tongues. This can give addicts a sixteen-hour high, but it can be very deadly.

The flying snake of Java and Malaysia is able to flatten itself out like a ribbon and sail like a glider from tree to tree.

Surviving all dangers, a wild cobra may live up to twenty years.

WHAT'S IN A NAME?

A group of finches is called a charm.

A group of frogs is called an army.

A group of geese on the ground is called a gaggle; a group of geese in the air is a skein.

A group of goats is called a trip.

A group of hares is called a husk.

A group of kangaroos is called a mob.

A group of owls is called a parliament.

A group of rhinos is called a crash.

A group of toads is called a knot.

We speak of a bale of turtles, a clowder of cats, a gam of whales, and a streak of tigers.

MONKEY BUSINESS

Thirty thousand monkeys were used in the massive three-year effort to classify the various types of polio.

Scientific researchers say promiscuous species of monkeys appear to have stronger immune systems than less sexually active ones.

Male monkeys lose the hair on their heads in the same manner men do.

The howler monkey is the loudest animal living in the rain forests of South America. Their voices can be heard up to five miles away.

A male chimpanzee is five times hornier than the average human.

Apart from humans, certain species of chimpanzee are the only animals to experiment sexually. They have been known to "wife swap" and indulge in group sex.

Just like people, mother chimpanzees often develop lifelong relationships with their offspring.

Gorillas beat their chests when they get nervous.

Gorillas often sleep for up to fourteen hours a day.

Human birth control pills work on gorillas.

The scientific name for a gorilla is *Gorilla gorilla gorilla*.

There is a strong bond between mother and child among orangutans. Orangutan infants cling almost continually to their mothers until they are one year old.

To warn off other males, the orangutans of Southeast Asia burp loudly to declare their territory.

PIG OUT

It is physically impossible for pigs to look up at the sky.

Scientists say that pigs, unlike all other domestic animals, arrive at solutions by thinking them through. Pigs can be—and have been—taught to accomplish almost any feat a dog can master, and usually in a shorter period of time.

The Duroc is an American breed of hardy hog that has droopy ears. It was allegedly named after the horse owned by the hog's breeder.

GOING BATTY

The more that is learned about the ecological benefits of bats, the more home gardeners are going out of their way to entice these amazing winged mammals into their neighborhoods. Bats are voracious insect eaters, devouring as many as six hundred bugs per hour for four to six hours a night. They can eat from one-half to three-quarters their weight per evening. Bats are also important plant pollinators, particularly in the southwestern United States.

Bats are the only mammals that can fly.

Bats can live up to thirty years or more.

Bats always turn left when exiting a cave.

The leg bones of a bat are so thin that no bat can walk.

Worldwide, bats are the most important natural enemies of night-flying insects.

The nearly one thousand kinds of bats account for almost a quarter of all mammal species, and most are highly beneficial.

The twenty million Mexican free-tailed bats from Bracken Cave, Texas, eat approximately two hundred tons of insects nightly.

Mexican free-tailed bats sometimes fly up to two miles high to feed or to catch tailwinds that carry them over long distances at speeds of more than sixty miles per hour.

Vampire bats adopt orphans and have been known to risk their lives to share food with less-fortunate roost-mates.

Vampire bats don't suck blood; they drink it. They make small cuts in the skin of a sleeping animal, and while their saliva numbs the area, the bat laps up the blood. Vampire bats need about two tablespoonfuls of blood each day. The creature is able to extract its dinner in approximately twenty minutes.

Red bats that live in tree foliage throughout most of North America can withstand body temperatures as low as 23 degrees Fahrenheit during winter hibernation.

The pallid bat of western North America is immune to the stings of scorpions as well as the seven-inch centipedes upon which it feeds.

The Honduran white bat is snow white with a yellow nose and ears. It cuts large leaves to make "tents" that protect its small colonies from jungle rains.

Tiny woolly bats in West Africa live in the large webs of colonial spiders.

The brown myotis bat's young when born are equivalent to a woman giving birth to a thirty-pound baby.

Disc-winged bats of Latin America have adhesive discs on both wings and feet that enable them to live in unfurling banana leaves (or even to walk up a window pane!).

MISSING IN ACTION

Dinosaurs were among the most sophisticated animals that ever lived on Earth. They survived for nearly 150 million years—seventy-five times longer than humans have now lived on Earth.

> There were two main types of dinosaurs. Saurischia dinosaurs had hip and pelvic bones like lizards and consisted of meat- and plant-eating dinosaurs. Ornithischia dinosaurs had hip and pelvic bones like birds and consisted of small plant-eaters.

Time and erosion have erased 99 percent of all dinosaur footprints.

> Most published species of dinosaurs have been published within the last twenty years.

Some dinosaurs were as small as hens.

> The first dinosaur appeared around 225 or 230 million years ago. It was called the Staurikosaurus, and it survived for about five million years.

The first dinosaur to be given a name was the Iguanodon, found in Sussex, United Kingdom, in 1823. It was not the first dinosaur to be found. The first dinosaur to be found and recognized as a huge reptile was the Megalosaurus.

Sue, the world's largest, most complete, and best preserved Tyrannosaurus Rex, made her grand debut to the public on May 17, 2000, at the Field Museum in Chicago, Illinois.

The first flying animals were the pterosaurs that appeared more than two hundred million years ago. They were closer to flying reptiles than birds.

The ancient nautilus is considered the most intelligent of the invertebrates; it is said to have been as intelligent as a young cat.

The woolly mammoth, extinct since the Ice Age, had tusks almost sixteen feet long.

The dodo, extinct less than one hundred years after being discovered by the Dutch in 1598, was not a prolific species. The female laid just one egg a year.

BAMBI AND FRIENDS

Deer cannot eat hay. They do like to eat marijuana.

In 1978, more deer were killed by Connecticut automobile drivers than by Connecticut hunters.

There are no wild deer of any kind in Australia, and the small red deer is the only one found in Africa.

Reindeer have scent glands between their hind toes. The glands help them leave scent trails for the herd. Researchers say the odor smells cheesy.

Reindeer like to eat bananas.

The Latin name for moose is *alces alces*.

The Alaskan moose is the largest deer in North America. It attains a height at the withers in excess of seven feet and, when fully grown, weighs up to eighteen hundred pounds.

The antlers of a male moose can have as many as thirty tines, or spikes.

The male moose sheds its antlers every winter and grows a new set the following year.

The antlers of a moose are created from living tissue supplied by blood through a network of vessels covered with a soft smooth skin called velvet. Eventually, the tissue becomes solidified, the velvet is scraped off, and the antlers become completely formed of dead matter.

Moose have very poor vision. Some have even tried to mate with cars.

The cells that make up moose antlers are the fastest-growing animal cells in nature.

The only female animal that has antlers is the caribou. There are more caribou in Alaska than there are people.

LIONS AND TIGERS AND . . .

The two best-known cat noises are roaring and purring. Only four species can roar, and they don't purr: lions, leopards, tigers, and jaguars.

Lions are the only truly social cat species, and usually every female in a pride, ranging from five to thirty individuals, is closely related.

Lions sleep up to twenty hours a day.

It is the female lion who does more than 90 percent of the hunting, while the male is afraid to risk his life, or simply prefers to rest.

Due to a retinal adaptation that reflects light to the retina, the night vision of tigers is six times better than that of humans.

> Between 1902 and 1907, the same tiger killed 436 people in India.

Tigers have striped skin, not just striped fur.

> Tiger cubs are born blind and weigh only about two to three pounds, depending on the subspecies. They live on milk for six to eight weeks before the female begins taking them to kills to feed. Tigers have fully developed canines by sixteen months of age, but they do not begin making their own kills until about eighteen months of age.

Tigers have stripes to help them hide in the rain forest undergrowth. The black and gold stripes break up the outline of the tiger's body, making it very hard to see.

> The cheetah can reach a speed of up to forty-five miles per hour in only two seconds.

Running in short bursts, the cheetah can reach a speed of sixty-two miles per hour.

> There is no single cat called the panther. The name is commonly applied to the leopard, but it is also used to

refer to the puma and the jaguar. A black panther is really a black leopard.

Belize is the only country in the world with a jaguar reserve.

Jaguars are scared of dogs.

Cats have more than one hundred vocal sounds, while dogs only have about ten.

The domestic cat is the only species able to hold its tail vertically while walking. Wild cats hold their tails horizontally or tucked between their legs while walking.

Despite its reputation for being finicky, the average cat consumes about 130,000 calories a year, nearly twenty times its own weight in food and the same amount again in liquids. In case you were wondering, cats cannot survive on a vegetarian diet.

Kittens are born both blind and deaf, but the vibration of their mother's purring is a physical signal that the kittens can feel—it acts like a homing device, signaling them to nurse.

Kittens can clock an amazing thirty-one miles per hour at full speed and can cover about three times their body length per leap.

Rome has more homeless cats per square mile than any other city in the world.

 ## . . . BEARS, OH MY!

There are seven species of bears: the American black bear, the Asian black bear, the brown bear, the polar bear, the sloth bear, the spectacled bear, and the sun bear.

The Kodiak grizzly bear is the world's largest meat-eating animal living on land. The Kodiak can weigh up to five hundred pounds more than any other kind of bear.

The grizzly bear is capable of running as fast as the average horse.

The most carnivorous of all bears is the polar bear. Its diet consists almost entirely of seals and fish.

Polar bears have more problems with overheating than they do with cold. Even in very cold weather, they quickly overheat when they try to run.

The polar bear is the only bear that has hair on the soles of its feet. This protects the animal's feet from the cold and prevents slipping on the ice.

At birth, a panda is smaller than a mouse and weighs about four ounces.

MISTAKEN IDENTITY

Koalas are marsupials, not bears. They also have no tail or eyelids.

Mountain goats are not goats. They are small antelopes.

The jackrabbit is not a rabbit; it is a hare.

The killer whale is not a whale but the largest member of the dolphin family.

RODENT RIDDLES

A rodent's teeth never stop growing. They are worn down by the animal's constant gnawing on bark, leaves, and other vegetables.

The mouse is the most common mammal in the United States.

According to Dr. David Gems, a British geneticist, sex-craved male mice, which spend five to eleven hours per day pursuing female mice, could live years longer if they abstained.

Mice will nurse babies that are not their own.

More than a third of the field mice in the Kesterson National Wildlife refuge near Los Banos, California, have both male and female reproductive organs.

There are mice that nest in trees. These creatures may spend their whole lives without ever touching the ground.

There are species of mice that live in marshy places and are excellent swimmers.

The typical laboratory mouse runs five miles per night on its treadmill.

A rat can last longer without water than a camel.

Rats can't vomit.

Rats can swim for a half mile without resting, and they can tread water for three days straight.

Two rats can become the progenitors of fifteen thousand rats in less than a year.

Unlike most female animals, the female rice rat is the one that searches for and pursues a mate.

Kangaroo rats never drink water. Like their relatives the pocket mice, they carry their own water source within them, producing fluids from the food they eat and the air they breathe.

Eleven chinchillas were brought from the Andes Mountains in South America in the 1930s. All chinchillas presently in North America are descended from these eleven chinchillas.

The large hind feet of the chinchilla help it hop like a kangaroo, and its small front legs and feet are similar to those of a squirrel.

Many hamsters only blink one eye at a time.

Reportedly, beavers mate for life.

The groundhog is a member of the rodent family. The typical adult groundhog can weigh approximately eight to fourteen pounds and average about twenty-two inches in length.

CREATURES OF THE SKY

The *Practitioner*, a British medical journal, has determined that bird-watching may be hazardous to your health. The magazine, in fact, has officially designated bird-watching a hazardous hobby, after documenting the death of a weekend bird-watcher who became so immersed in his subject that he grew oblivious to his surroundings and, consequently, was eaten by a crocodile.

The eyes of some birds weigh more than their brains. Likewise, their bones weigh less than their feathers.

The optimum depth of water in a birdbath is two-and-a-half inches. Less water makes it difficult for birds to take a bath; more makes them afraid.

The five fastest birds are: the peregrine falcon that can fly up to 175 miles per hour, the spine-tailed swift that can go 106 miles per hour, the frigate bird at 95 miles per hour, the spur-winged goose at 88 miles per hour, and the red-breasted merganser at 80 miles per hour.

To survive, most birds must eat at least half their own weight in food each day.

Some species of rain forest birds migrate every summer from South America to Canada to breed.

Mallard nests are sometimes built at a height of forty feet above ground.

Herons have been observed to drop insects on the water and then catch the fish that surface for the bugs.

The American woodcock, with its eyes placed toward the top of its head, can see backward and upward, and forward and upward, with binocular vision and, laterally, almost 180 degrees with each eye.

The male argus pheasant of Asia has the longest feathers of all the flying birds. Its tail feathers can reach a length of six feet.

Roosters cannot crow if they can't fully extend their necks.

The Everglades kite bird, in Florida, will only eat apple snails. The kites are becoming rare because as the Everglades dry up, the apple snails are dying out.

The female knot-tying weaverbird will refuse to mate with a male who has built a shoddy nest. If spurned, the male must take the nest apart and completely rebuild it to win the affections of the female.

Migrating geese fly in a V formation to conserve energy. A goose's wings churn the air and leave an air current behind. In the flying wedge, each bird is in position to get a lift from the current left by the bird ahead. It is easier going for all except the leader. During a migration, geese are apt to take turns in the lead position.

The female pigeon cannot lay eggs if she is alone. For her ovaries to function, she must be able to see another pigeon. If no other pigeon is available, her own reflection in a mirror will suffice.

The kiwi, national bird of New Zealand, can't fly. It lives in a hole in the ground, is almost blind, and lays only one egg each year. Despite this, it has survived for more than seventy million years.

The penduline titmouse of Africa builds its home in such a sturdy manner that Masai tribesman use their nests for purses and carrying cases.

The pitohui bird of Papua New Guinea has enough poison in its feathers and skin to kill mice and frogs. The poison can affect humans, often causing them numbness, burning, and sneezing.

Domesticated turkeys (farm-raised) cannot fly. Wild turkeys can fly for short distances at up to fifty-five miles per hour. Wild turkeys are also fast on the ground, running at speeds of up to thirty miles per hour.

The heaviest bird in the world is the Kori bustard. The Kori weighs around thirty-one pounds on average, but the largest one found was more than forty pounds.

Although the Connecticut warbler passes through Connecticut only on its autumn migration, this shy, seldom-seen songbird bears the name of the state where it was first collected by pioneer ornithologist Alexander Wilson in 1812.

The acorn woodpecker leaves its food sticking out of the holes it's drilled in oak trees, making it easy for squirrels and jays to help themselves.

The life expectancy of the average mockingbird is ten years.

The loudest bird in the world is the male bellbird, found in Central and South America. To attract mates, the male makes a clanging sound like a bell that can be heard from miles away.

There are seven distinctive types of combs on chickens: rose, strawberry, single, cushion, buttercup, pea, and V shaped.

There are more than 450 species of finches throughout the world.

The emu is Australia's largest bird at a height of seven feet tall. It can't fly, but it can swim and has the ability to run up to forty miles per hour.

The female condor lays a single egg once every two years.

The pelican breathes through its mouth because it has no nostrils.

Male cockatoos can be taught to speak, but females can only chirp and sing.

♟ SWAN SONG

The queen (or more precisely the Royal Household) owns all swans in England. The post of Royal Swankeeper is a post that has been around since 1215, and he and his staff are responsible for keeping accurate statistics about the number and whereabouts of the royal swans.

During the 1800s, swan skins were used to make European ladies' powder puffs and swan feathers were used to adorn fashionable hats.

Many seabirds that swallow fishes too large for immediate digestion go about with the esophagus filled. Apparently without discomfort, the tail of the fish sticks out of the bird's mouth.

Seabirds have salt-excreting organs above their eyes that enable them to drink saltwater; sea snakes have a similar filter at the base of their tongues.

The grebe, an aquatic bird, has an effective means of escaping danger while protecting its young. At the first sign of danger, it will sink into the water until its back is level with the surface. This allows its offspring to swim over and quickly climb on to its back. The parent grebe then rises up to its swimming position and ferries the chicks across the water to safety.

The albatross can glide on air currents for several days and can even sleep while in flight.

The albatross drinks sea water. It has a special desalinization apparatus that strains out and excretes all excess salt.

In Miami, Florida, roosting vultures have taken to snatching poodles from rooftop patios.

The Egyptian vulture, a white bird about the size of a raven, throws stones with its beak to open ostrich eggs to eat. This bird is one of the very few animals that, like man, manipulates objects as tools.

There are more than three hundred species of parrots.

Macaws are the largest and most colorful species of the parrot family.

> The nest of the African Grey Parrot is a hole in a large tree. The bird uses no nesting material. It lays its eggs in the wood dust at the bottom of the nest holes, which are about two to six feet deep.

The owl parrot can't fly and builds its nest under tree roots.

> The horned owl is not horned. Two tufts of feathers were mistaken for horns.

The owl is the only bird to drop its upper eyelid to wink. All other birds raise their lower eyelids.

> To see at night as well as an owl, you would need eyeballs as big as grapefruits.

The great horned owl can turn its head 270 degrees.

> The European eagle owl is the largest owl in the world. It can measure twenty-eight inches tall with a wingspan of five feet wide.

Ducks will lay eggs only in the early morning.

> A duck has three eyelids.

A sheep, a duck, and a rooster were the first passengers in a hot air balloon.

The largest bird egg in the world today is that of the ostrich. Ostrich eggs are from six to eight inches long. Because of their size and the thickness of their shells, they take forty minutes to hard-boil.

There is just one known species of ostrich in the world—it is in the order of *Struthioniformes.*

The ostrich has only two toes, unlike most birds, which have three or four.

The ostrich has four eyelids. The inner lids are for blinking and keeping the eyeballs moist, the outer lids for casting come-hither glances at potential mates.

An ostrich's eye is bigger than its brain.

To keep cool, ostriches urinate on their legs; it then evaporates like sweat.

Eagles can live in captivity for up to forty-six years.

South America's harpy eagles eat monkeys. The birds build twig platforms in the treetops where they lay their eggs.

The African eagle, swooping at more than one hundred miles per hour, can brake to a halt in twenty feet.

The nest of the bald eagle can weigh well over a ton.

Eagles mate while airborne.

The hum of a hummingbird comes from the super-fast beat of the wings. The smallest ones beat their wings the fastest—up to eighty times per second. Even the slower beat of bigger hummingbirds' wings is so fast you can only see a blur.

The hummingbird is the only bird that can fly backward.

It would require an average of eighteen hummingbirds to weigh in at one ounce. The hummingbird's tiny brain, 4.2 percent of its body weight, is proportionately the largest in the bird kingdom.

Flamingos are pink because they consume vast quantities of algae.

Flamingos can live up to eighty years.

Flamingos can only eat with their heads upside down.

MARCH OF THE PENGUINS

The penguin is the only bird that can swim but not fly. It is also the only bird that walks upright. Earlier penguins were capable of flight.

Penguins do not tip over when an airplane flies over them.

The deepest penguin dive was 1,261 feet under the water.

The emperor penguin is the largest type of penguin. It is also the deepest diver, reaching depths of 870 feet and staying there for up to 18 minutes.

The Adélie penguin bears the name of French explorer Dumont d'Urville's beloved wife.

There are no penguins at the North Pole. In fact, there are no penguins anywhere in the Northern Hemisphere (outside of zoos). All seventeen varieties of the bird are found below the equator, primarily in Antarctica.

UNDER THE SEA

There are more species of fish than mammals, reptiles, and birds combined.

The pair of fins at the back of a fish's body are called pelvic fins.

More species of fish live in a single tributary of the Amazon River than in all the rivers in North America combined.

Sturgeon can live as long as one hundred years, reaching sexual maturity in the wild at around fifteen to twenty years of age. Mature females will produce millions of eggs every two to three years.

The garfish has green bones.

The longest fish is the oarfish, which is shaped like an eel. On average, it grows to more than twenty feet in length, but oarfish of forty-six feet have been found.

The African lungfish can live without water for up to four years. When a drought occurs, it digs a pit and encloses itself in a capsule of slime and earth, leaving a small opening for breathing. The capsule dries and hardens, but the fish is protected. When rain comes, the capsule dissolves and the lungfish swims away.

Minnows have teeth in their throats.

The candlefish is so oily that it was once burned for fuel.

The flounder swims sideways.

The mudskipper fish can actually walk on land.

Many types of fish—called mouthbrooders—carry their eggs in their mouths until the babies hatch and can care for themselves.

The Mola mola, or ocean sunfish, lays up to five million eggs at one time.

Walking catfish of Florida can stay out of water for eighty days.

Lungless salamanders are the largest group of salamanders. They have no lungs or gills and breathe through their skin, which must be kept damp to allow in oxygen. If they dry out, they will die of suffocation.

The gurnard, a fish found in Florida, grunts when a thunderstorm is brewing. It's said to be more reliable than meteorologists.

Sea sponges are used in drugs for treating asthma and cancer.

The glue of a barnacle cannot be dissolved with strong acids or temperatures set as high as 440 degrees Fahrenheit.

A four-inch-long abalone can grip a rock with a force of four hundred pounds. Two grown men are incapable of prying it loose.

A winkle is an edible sea snail.

Only 30 percent of the famous Maryland blue crab are actually from Maryland; the rest are from North Carolina and Virginia.

A scallop has a total of thirty-five eyes, which are all blue.

The largest species of seahorse measures eight inches.

A shrimp has more than a hundred pairs of chromosomes in each cell nucleus. The shrimp's heart is in its head.

Shrimp swim backward.

The minuscule krill shrimp has eleven pairs of legs.

The pistol shrimp makes a noise so loud it can shatter glass.

Some mantis shrimp travel by doing backward somersaults.

Tuna swim at a steady rate of nine miles per hour for an indefinite period of time—and they never stop moving. Estimates indicate that a fifteen-year-old tuna travels one million miles in its lifetime.

Tuna will suffocate if they ever stop swimming. They need a continual flow of water across their gills to breathe, even while they rest.

FREE WILLY

The killer whale, or orca, is the fastest sea mammal. It can reach speeds up to thirty-four miles per hour in pursuit of prey.

Measuring about eight feet at birth, killer whale bulls can grow to twenty-five feet and weigh as much as six tons.

It seems to biologists that, unlike their humpback whale relatives, whose underwater song evolves from year to year, killer whales retain individual dialects unchanged over long periods, possibly even for life.

The humpback whale's flippers grow to a maximum of 31 percent of its body length—that's a potential maximum length of about eighteen feet. Because of these enormous flippers, the whale's Latin name translates to "big-winged New Englander."

A forty-two-foot sperm whale has about seven tons of oil in it.

The gray whale is not really gray. It is black and just appears gray from a distance. It has a series of up to 180 fringed overlapping plates hanging from each side of its upper jaw. This is where teeth would be located if the creature had any.

Electric eels are not really eels but a kind of fish. Although they look like eels, their internal organs are arranged differently. Unlike most fish, electric eels cannot get enough oxygen from water. Approximately every five minutes, they must surface to breathe or they will drown. Unlike most fish, they can swim both backward and forward.

> The electric eel has thousands of electric cells running up and down its tail. Vital body organs, such as the heart, are packed into a small space behind the head. They use their electric sense to "see." Their electric sensors act like radar, sending out weak impulses that bounce off objects.

The electric eel is the most shocking animal on Earth—no other animal packs such a big charge. If attacking large prey, a nine-foot-long eel can discharge about eight hundred volts. One zap could stun a human. The larger the eel, the bigger the charge.

> The electric organs in an electric eel make up four-fifths of its body.

The adult electric eel has enough electrical power in it to power a house of about twelve hundred square feet. The average discharge is four hundred volts.

> Some species of freshwater eels migrate to the Sargasso Sea in the Atlantic Ocean to mate. After laying

up to twenty million eggs, the female eel dies. The baby eels hatched from the eggs then make their way back to fresh water.

The Portuguese man-of-war is found most commonly in the Gulf Stream of the northern Atlantic Ocean and in the tropical and subtropical regions of the Indian and Pacific Oceans. It is sometimes found floating in groups numbering in the thousands. Its "jellyfish" tentacles have been known to grow a mile in length, catching anything in its path by stinging its prey.

The lethal Lion's Mane jellyfish has a bell reaching up to eight feet in diameter and tentacles longer than a blue whale—up to two hundred feet long. Juveniles are pink, turning red as they mature, and then becoming brownish purple when adults.

The beautiful but deadly Australian sea wasp (*Chironex fleckeri*) is the most venomous jellyfish in the world. Its cardiotoxic venom has caused the deaths of sixty-six people off the coast of Queensland since 1880, with victims dying within one to three minutes if medical aid is not available.

Jellyfish are comprised of more than 95 percent water and have no brain, heart, or bones and no actual eyes.

Coral are closely related to jellyfish.

The leather coral, which is softer than the stony coral, may attack and eat one of its own kind if subjected to crowded conditions.

Schools of South American (Pacific) Humboldt squid, which reach twelve feet in length, have been known to strip five-hundred-pound marlins to the bone.

Scientists still know very little about the giant squid, except what can be gleaned from the carcasses of about one hundred beached squid dating back to 1639. Despite centuries of myths and exciting tales of sightings of giant squid, more information is known about dinosaurs.

Scientists do know that giant squid have eyes as big as watermelons.

To a human, one giant octopus looks virtually the same as any other of the same size and species. This explains why divers claim to have seen the same octopus occupy a den for ten or more years. But an octopus seldom lives longer than four years.

An octopus will eat its own arms if it gets really hungry.

The octopus's testicles are located in its head. The pupil of an octopus's eye is rectangular.

Using its web—the skin between its arms—an octopus can carry up to a dozen crabs back to its den.

The oyster is usually ambisexual. It begins life as a male, becomes a female, then changes back to a male, then back to a female. It may go back and forth many times.

No pearls of value are ever found in North American oysters.

It can take a deep-sea clam up to one hundred years to reach a third of an inch in length. The clam is among the slowest-growing yet longest-living species on the planet. The quahog, a marine clam, can live for up to two hundred years, making it the longest-living ocean creature in the world. Second place goes to the killer whale at ninety years; third is the blue whale at eighty years; fourth is the sea turtle at fifty years; and fifth is the tiger shark at forty years.

Lobsters, like grasshoppers, feel no pain. They have a decentralized nervous system with no cerebral cortex, which in humans is where a reaction to painful stimuli proceeds.

Lobsters molt twenty to thirty times before reaching the one-pound market size. This takes approximately seven years.

You can cut up a starfish into pieces, and each piece will grow into a completely new starfish.

Some species of starfish have as many as fifty appendages.

Starfish feed on mollusks and crustaceans. In some areas, they are a serious threat to oyster and clam beds.

Starfish have eyespots at the tip of each arm. These act as light sensors and contain a red pigment that changes chemically in the presence of light. The eyespots are believed to influence the starfish's behavior, particularly movement.

Dolphins do not breathe automatically, as humans do, and so they do not sleep as humans do. If they became unconscious, they would sink to the bottom of the sea. Without the oxygen they need to take in periodically, they would die.

Dolphins swim in circles while they sleep, with the eye on the outside of the circle open to keep watch for predators. After a certain amount of time, they reverse and swim in the opposite direction with the opposite eye open.

Dolphins jump out of the water to conserve energy. It is easier to move through the air than through the water.

Dolphins have killed sharks by ramming them with their snouts.

JAWS!

Sharks' fossil records date back more than twice as far as those of the dinosaurs.

Sharks can travel up to forty miles per hour.

Sharks have a sixth sense that enables them to detect bio-electrical fields radiated by other sea creatures and to navigate by sensing changes in the earth's magnetic field.

Sharks and rays are the only animals known to man that cannot succumb to cancer. Scientists believe this is related to the fact that they have no bone, only cartilage.

Some sharks swim in a figure eight when frightened.

Sharks can be dangerous even before they are born. Scientist Stewart Springer was bitten by a sand tiger shark embryo while he was examining its pregnant mother.

The enormous livers of basking sharks, which can account for up to one-third of their body weight, produce valuable oil used to lubricate engines and manufacture cosmetics.

The largest great white shark ever caught measured thirty-seven feet and weighed twenty-four thousand pounds. It was found in a herring weir in New Brunswick in 1930.

The great distance between the eyes and nostrils of the hammerhead shark may allow the animal to detect its prey's direction more accurately. They are experts at catching the stingrays on which they feed.

The nurse shark spends much of its time in caves. It leaves the security of its cave to feed on prey such as lobsters, squid, and crabs. The sucking sound of its powerful throat muscles is probably the origin of the animal's common name.

The hides of mature female blue sharks are more than twice as thick as those of males, probably as a protection against courtship bites.

Lemon sharks grow a new set of teeth every two weeks. They grow more than twenty-four thousand new teeth every year.

The harmless whale shark holds the title of largest fish, with the record being a fifty-nine-footer captured in Thailand in 1919.

CIRCUS PERFORMERS

There once were more sea lions on Earth than people.

Male sea lions may have more than one hundred wives and sometimes go three months without eating.

The rare Hawaiian monk seal has been known to dive to about 1,650 feet. The animal doesn't "bark" like sea lions, but has a number of different vocalizations it produces, including a deep, guttural call that sounds much like a belch. Seals and whales keep warm in the icy polar water thanks to a layer of fat called blubber under their skin. Whale blubber can reach up to twenty inches thick.

Seals can sleep underwater and surface for air without even waking.

The elephant seal is the heaviest seal in the world; males can reach twenty feet in length and eighty-eight hundred pounds.

Researchers have determined that the elephant seals off the Baja coast dive deeper than whales—sometimes as deep as a mile.

Seals can withstand water pressure of up to 850 pounds per square inch.

Seals have back flippers that can't bend under the body to "walk" on land, while sea lions use their leg-like hind flippers to "walk" on land.

Fur seals get miserably sick when they're carried aboard ships.

Seals must teach their young how to swim.

The Weddell seal can travel underwater for seven miles without surfacing for air.

🐾 HUNGRY, HUNGRY HIPPOS

The hippopotamus is, next to the elephant, the heaviest of all land mammals. It may weigh as much as eight thousand pounds. It is also a close relative of the pig. It has skin an inch and a half thick; it's so solid that most bullets cannot penetrate it.

The hippopotamus has the world's shortest sperm.

The hippopotamus gives birth underwater and nurses its young in the river as well, although the young hippos must come up periodically for air. Hippopotami cannot swim.

Sea otters have the world's densest fur—a million hairs per square inch.

Sea otters inhabit water but never get wet because they have two coats of fur.

It is estimated that manatees live a maximum of fifty to sixty years.

DOGGY STYLE

There are more than one hundred million dogs and cats in the United States

Dogs that do not tolerate small children well include the Saint Bernard, the Old English sheepdog, the Alaskan malamute, the bull terrier, and the toy poodle.

Studies show that the breeds of dogs that bite the least are, in order: the golden retriever, Labrador retriever, Shetland sheepdog, Old English sheepdog, and the Welsh terrier.

The only dog to ever appear in a Shakespearean play was Crab in *The Two Gentlemen of Verona.*

The onomatopoeia for a dog's bark in Japanese is "wan-wan."

The fastest dog, the greyhound, can reach speeds of up to forty-five miles per hour. The breed was known to exist in ancient Egypt more than five thousand years ago.

The prescribed diet of the Polish lowland sheepdog in present-day Poland consists of bread, potatoes, cottage cheese, milk, and an occasional egg.

The New Guinea singing dog's most unique characteristic is its dramatic ability to vary the pitch of its howl. The animal does not bark repetitively but has a complex vocal behavior, including yelps, whines, and single-note howls.

Terrier is from the Latin word *terra* meaning "earth."

Though human noses have an impressive 5 million olfactory cells with which to smell, sheepdogs have 220 million, enabling them to smell 44 times better than man.

Jackals have one more pair of chromosomes than dogs or wolves.

The gray wolf is the largest wild dog alive today. As an adult a gray wolf can weigh up to 176 pounds.

There is no record of a nonrabid wolf attack on a human.

The last wolf in Great Britain was killed in Scotland, in 1743. Wolves were extinct in England by 1500.

To safeguard its food when away, the wolverine marks it with a strong musk so foul smelling that other animals won't touch it.

Very unusual for carnivores, hyena clans are dominated by females.

ELEPHANTS ON PARADE

The elephant is the only mammal that can't jump.

Elephants perform greeting ceremonies when a member of the group returns after a long time away. The welcoming animals spin around, flap their ears, and trumpet.

Elephants communicate in sound waves below the frequency humans can hear.

Elephants have been known to remain standing after they die. It takes eleven truckloads of wood to make a proper funeral pyre for a full-sized elephant.

Elephants and short-tailed shrews get by on only two hours of sleep a day.

The massive skeleton of the African elephant accounts for about 15 percent of its body weight, just as in a man of slender build; however, the elephant's skeleton supports as much as four tons per leg, and is thus stressed close to the physical limit for bone. To keep from damaging its skeleton, an African elephant has to move sedately, never jumping or running. The "charge" of these animals is a fast walk on long legs, at about fifteen miles per hour.

Until he's about twenty-one years old, the male Indian elephant isn't interested in romancing a female elephant.

The elephant's closest relative is the hyrax, which is found in the Middle East and Africa and is only about one foot long. Like its gigantic cousin, the hyrax has hoofed toes and a two-chambered stomach for digesting a vegetable diet.

HORSING AROUND

There are more than 150 breeds of horses in the world.

The part of the foot of a horse between the fetlock and the hoof is called the pastern.

Today's oldest form of horse is the Przewalski, or Mongolian Wild Horse. Survivors of this breed were discovered in the Gobi Desert in 1881.

Thoroughbred horses are so thin-skinned their veins are visible beneath the skin, especially on the legs.

Though small, the Shetland pony is strong. It was once used to haul heavy cars in coal mines.

The normal body temperature of the Clydesdale horse is 101 degrees Fahrenheit.

With nearly eleven million horses within its borders, China is the leader of all nations for horse population.

Racehorses have been known to wear out new shoes in one race.

The now-extinct ancestor of the horse, the eohippus, had a short neck and a pug muzzle and stood no higher than a medium-sized dog.

Rhinos are in the same family as horses and are thought to have inspired the myth of the unicorn. A rhinoceros's horn is made of compacted hair.

STRANGE SPECIES

A geep is a cross between a goat and a sheep.

The only purple animal is the South African Blesbok.

The world's smallest mammal is the bumblebee bat of Thailand, weighing less than a penny.

There have been more than fifteen hundred documented sightings of Bigfoot since 1958.

The largest known egg ever laid by a creature was that of the extinct Aepyornis of Madagascar. The egg was nine and a half inches long.

The pichiciego is a little-known burrowing South American animal that is related to the armadillo but is smaller in size. The ending of the animal's name is derived from the Spanish word *ciego*, meaning "blind."

Unrelated to the chicken, the male cock-of-the-rock bird earned the name "cock" because of its roosterlike appearance and combative behavior. The female of the species influenced the word *rock* being added to the name because of her habit of nesting and rearing the young in sheltered rock niches.

HUMP DAY

The world camel population is approximately twenty million.

The longest recorded life span of a camel was thirty-five years, five months.

A camel's backbone is just as straight as a horse's.

Camel's milk does not curdle.

Camels have three eyelids to protect their eyes from blowing sand.

Traveling at a rate of two to three miles per hour, camels can carry five hundred to one thousand pounds on their backs. They are able to keep up this pace for six or seven hours a day. Camels will refuse to carry loads that are not properly balanced.

There are fewer than one thousand Bactrian camels left in the wild. They have survived in a land with no water in an area used for nuclear testing. Their numbers, however, are falling dramatically as humans encroach farther and farther into China's Gobi Desert.

The fur of the vicuna, a small member of the camel family that lives in the Andes Mountains of Peru, is so fine that each hair is less than two-thousandths of an inch thick. The animal was considered sacred by the Incas, and only royalty could wear its fleece.

THEY MIGHT BE GIANTS

There are fewer than one thousand giant pandas left alive in the world.

The giant African snail grows to a foot long and reaches weights greater than a pound.

The giant armadillo has as many as one hundred teeth, although they are small and fragile.

The giant flying foxes that live in Indonesia have wingspans of nearly six feet.

Giant tortoises can live to be 150 years old or older.

The giant Pacific octopus can fit its entire body through an opening no bigger than the size of its beak.

The giant squid is the largest creature without a backbone. It weighs up to two and a half tons and grows up to fifty-five feet long. Each eye is a foot or more in diameter.

TALL TALES

Mice, whales, elephants, giraffes, and humans all have seven neck vertebrae.

The gait of the giraffe is a pace, with both legs on one side moving together. Because of its long stride, a giraffe is quicker than it appears. At full gallop, the animal can run about thirty miles per hour.

The giraffe's heart is huge; it weighs twenty-five pounds, is two feet long, and has walls up to three inches thick. Thinking that a giraffe was a cross between a camel and a leopard, the Europeans once called the animal a camelopard.

THE TORTOISE AND THE HARE

Turtles, tortoises, and terrapins do not have teeth. They have hard, horny jaws that are able to cut and tear food.

The gender of a sea turtle is determined by the temperature of the sand during egg incubation. Warm temperatures produce more females; cooler temperatures produce more males.

Turtles survived the upheavals of the last two hundred million years, including the great extinction episode that eliminated the dinosaurs. Now, about half of the world's turtle species face possible extinction—due in large part to a growing demand for turtles as a popular dining delicacy and a source of traditional medicines.

The female green turtle sheds tears as she lays her eggs on the beach. This washes sand particles out of her eyes and rids her body of excess salt.

The hare can travel up to forty-five miles per hour, whereas the rabbit can achieve an average speed of just thirty-five miles per hour.

Jackrabbits can reach a speed of fifty miles per hour and can leap as high as five feet. A twenty-inch adult can leap twenty feet in a single bound.

COUNTING SHEEP

A single sheep's fleece might well contain as many as twenty-six million fibers.

Lanolin, an essential ingredient of many expensive cosmetics, is, in its native form, a foul-smelling, waxy, tarlike substance extracted from the fleece of sheep.

There are close to one million sheep in Iceland.

The horns of a bighorn sheep can weigh forty pounds.

THE ULTIMATE SURVIVORS

Skunks have more than smell to protect themselves. They can withstand five times the snake venom that would kill a rabbit.

A donkey will sink in quicksand, but a mule won't.

A woodchuck normally breathes twenty-one hundred times an hour, but it only breathes ten times an hour while it is hibernating.

One species of antelope, the Sitatunga, can sleep underwater.

Porcupines are excellent swimmers because their quills are hollow.

The honey badger can withstand hundreds of African bee stings that would kill any other animal.

To keep from being separated while sleeping, sea otters tie themselves together with kelp, often drifting miles out to sea during the night.

An armadillo can walk underwater.

The hedgehog has a large muscle running along its stomach so it can pull its lithe body into a tight, prickly little ball for defense.

The koala is one of the few land animals that does not need to drink water to survive.

PICKY EATERS

The porcupine's love for salt often leads the animal to roadways or walkways where salt has been sprinkled to melt the ice. They will lick and gnaw on anything containing salt, such as saddles, canoe paddles, and axe handles.

There are more goats than cows in mountainous countries because goats can survive well by eating grass and other brush.

Anteaters prefer termites to ants. They don't have any teeth or jaws, and their sticky tongue measures more than a foot long.

The duckbill platypus of Australia can store up to six hundred worms in its large cheek pouches.

It takes a sloth two weeks to digest the food it eats.

Mongooses were brought to Hawaii to kill rats. This plan failed because rats are nocturnal while the mongoose hunts during the day.

Carnivorous animals will not eat another animal that has been hit by a lightning strike.

THE PETTING ZOO

Americans spend more than $5.4 billion on their pets each year.

Victorian society rejected the notion that pets were capable of feelings or expressing emotion.

The dog and the turkey were the only two domesticated animals in ancient Mexico.

Llamas are reported to be inquisitive, friendly animals. A llama greeting is marked by softly blowing on each other. According to animal experts, a soft blow to a person is the llama's way of saying hello.

Armadillos can be housebroken.

The goose was the first domesticated animal.

The guinea pig originated in South America.

MAN VERSUS NATURE

Until they were imported into the country, Australia did not have any members of the cat family, hoofed animals, apes, or monkeys.

The only country in the world that has a Bill of Rights for cows is India.

Each day, fishermen kill more than a hundred whales.

Woodpecker scalps, porpoise teeth, and giraffe tails have all been used as money.

The Kansas City Railroad used to stop their trains to allow the passengers to shoot at passing buffalo.

The average cost of rehabilitating a seal after the *Exxon Valdez* oil spill in Alaska was eighty thousand dollars.

There were about sixty million bison when the Europeans landed in America. By the 1880s, all but five hundred bison were killed. Today there are 350,000 bison in America.

Statistics

PLANES, TRAINS, AND AUTOMOBILES

Ten percent of frequent fliers say they never check their luggage when flying.

Traveling by air is the safest means of transportation. More people are killed by donkeys annually than are killed in plane crashes.

A car is stolen every thirty seconds in the United States.

The record for the world's worst driver is a toss-up between two candidates: first, a seventy-five-year-old man who received ten traffic tickets, drove on the wrong side of the road four times, committed four hit-and-run offenses, and caused six accidents—all within twenty minutes on October 15, 1966. Second, a sixty-two-year-old woman who failed her driving test forty times before passing it in August 1970 (by that time, she could no longer afford to buy a car).

Less than 1 percent of all road accidents in Canada involve a moose.

It would take more than 150 years to drive a car to the sun.

More than 10 percent of all the salt produced annually in the world is used to de-ice American roads.

Fifty-five percent of motorbike accidents happen on the weekend.

Most fatal car accidents happen on a Saturday.

DAILY ROUTINE

Children between the ages of two and seven color, on average, for twenty-eight minutes every day.

The average adult spends about twelve minutes in the shower.

The average four-year-old child asks more than four hundred questions a day.

The average person keeps old magazines for twenty-nine weeks before they throw them out.

The average person speaks about 31,500 words per day.

The average person spends about two years on the phone in a lifetime.

The average person will spend two weeks over their lifetime waiting for the traffic lights to change.

LEISURE TIME

Fifty-six percent of the video game market is adults.

Seventy percent of all boats sold are used in fishing.

Ninety percent of women who walk into a department store immediately turn to the right.

In Japan, 20 percent of all publications sold are comic books.

The longest kiss on record lasted 130 hours, 2 minutes.

The world record for carrying a milk bottle on your head is twenty-four miles.

Halifax, Nova Scotia, has the largest number of bars per capita of anywhere else in the world.

It is estimated that at any one time, 0.7 percent of the world's population are drunk.

COULD THERE BE A CONNECTION?

About one out of every seventy people who pick their nose actually eats their boogers.

Ninety-five percent of food poisoning cases are never reported.

CAUSE OF DEATH

You're more likely to be killed by a champagne cork than a poisonous spider.

Thirteen people a year are killed by vending machines falling on them.

Your statistical chance of being murdered is one in twenty thousand.

Odds of being killed by a dog are one in seven hundred thousand.

Odds of being killed by a tornado are one in two million.

Odds of being killed by falling out of bed are one in two million.

Odds of being killed in a car crash are one in five thousand.

Odds of dying in the bathtub are one in one million.

Of the 266 men who have been pope, 33 have died violently.

At 1.6 deaths for every 1,000 persons, Qatar has the lowest death rate in the world.

WEDDED BLISS

Two out of five husbands tell their wives daily that they love them.

About 6 percent of murdered American men are killed by either their wife or girlfriend . . . or their wife who caught them with their girlfriend.

Forty percent of women have hurled footwear at a man.

Thirty-five percent of the people who use personal ads for dating are already married.

Nobody has yet explained satisfactorily why couples who marry in January, February, and March tend to have the highest divorce rates.

Experienced waitresses say that married men tip better than unmarried men.

REPEAT OFFENDERS

One in ten people are arrested every year in the United States.

Women shoplift more often than men; the statistics are four to one.

Fifty percent of bank robberies take place on Fridays.

Chances that a burglary in the United States will be solved: one in seven.

About 43 percent of convicted criminals in the United States are rearrested within a year of being released from prison.

Sweden has the least number of murders annually.

The murder rate in the United States is two hundred times greater than in Japan. In Japan, no private citizen can buy a handgun legally.

PUBLIC OPINION

One out of four people do not know what their astrological sign is.

Fifty percent of teenage boys say they would rather be rich than smart.

Fifty-seven percent of British schoolkids think Germany is the most boring country in Europe.

Sixty-nine percent of men say they would rather break up with a girl in private than in public.

Seven percent of Americans think Elvis is alive.

Nine percent of Americans report having been in the presence of a ghost.

Only 55 percent of Americans know that the sun is a star.

More than 50 percent of Americans believe in the devil.

Percentage of men who say they are happier after their divorce or separation: 58 percent.

Percentage of women who say they are happier after their divorce or separation: 85 percent.

Eighty-two percent of the world's population believes in an afterlife.

About 5 percent of Americans claim to have talked to the devil personally.

BUT CAN YOU REMEMBER THEIR NAMES?

Assuming Rudolph was in front, there are 40,320 ways to rearrange the other eight reindeer.

BABY BOOMS

About two hundred babies are born worldwide every minute.

August is the month when most babies are born.

Twelve babies will be given to the wrong parents each day.

The world record for most children to one mother is sixty-nine children.

You share a birthday with at least nine million other people in the world.

There are about fifteen thousand people in the United States over the age of one hundred.

PLAYING IT SAFE

Statistically, the safest age of life is ten years old.

Summer is statistically the most hazardous season.

You are more likely to get attacked by a cow than a shark.

The percentage of men who wash their hands after using a toilet is 55 percent.

The percentage of women who wash their hands after using a toilet is 80 percent.

In the next seven days, eight hundred Americans will be injured by their jewelry.

Men are 1.6 times more likely to undergo bypass surgery than women.

EQUIPMENT FAILURE

Twenty-two thousand checks will be deducted from the wrong bank accounts in the next hour.

> An estimated 880,000 credit cards in circulation will turn out to have incorrect cardholder information on their magnetic strips.

About 811,000 faulty rolls of thirty-five millimeters film will be purchased this year.

THIS WAS ALL FOR NOTHING . . .

Approximately 97 percent of all statistics are made up.